641.8653 BRO

01209 616259

D0319788

Debbie Brown's

DREAM
Wedding Cakes

Introduction

When deciding to write this book, I wanted to put together a collection of dream wedding cakes, exquisitely detailed and contemporary for today's couples, yet all totally different. My aim was to bridge the gap between the fun, novelty type wedding cake and the traditional floral choice that is typically chosen for most wedding celebrations.

A beautifully designed and decorated cake is an extremely important focal point to any special wedding celebration. Not only should your cake look fantastic, it should taste wonderful too. This collection of cakes is stylish and contemporary, some funky and modern, a few romantic. As couples often opt for different cake flavours for each tier, I've also included some delicious recipes that will not disappoint.

If you're attempting to make your own wedding cake, there are clear step-by-step instructions and beautifully photographed stage work to help you along. If you don't have much cake decorating experience, I recommend you read through the guidance pages at the front of the book to ensure you understand the basics first, as to understand the recipes and the materials you are using is important to get the results you want for your special day. Some projects are quite involved, but for a special celebration they are well worth all the time and effort. Modelled items can be made well in advance to help manage time spent on the cake during the run-up to the wedding.

For experienced cake decorators who are looking for extra choices for their wedding couples, I hope you use this book to explore new ideas to broaden your special creativity, but also to give yourself a break from the enjoyable but relentless flower making that takes up so much of our time.

As usual I say, 'have fun,' which of course is what being creative is all about.

Debbie

Debbie Brown

For Lewis and Rachael, I wish them both all the happiness in the world.

First published in October 2008 by B. Dutton Publishing Limited, Alfred House, Hones Business Park, Farnham, Surrey, GU9 8BB.

Reprinted in May 2009 and February 2010.

Copyright: Debra Brown 2008

ISBN-13: 978-1-905113-10-1

All rights reserved.

No part of this publication may be reproduced, stored in a retrieval system or transmitted in any form or by means electronic, mechanical, photocopying, recording, or otherwise, without prior written permission of the copyright owner. A catalogue record of this book is available from the British Library.

Debbie Brown has asserted her right under the Copyright, Designs and Patents Act, 1988, to be identified as the author of this work.

CORNWALL COLLEGE
LEARNING CENTRE

All wallpapers supplied by **wallpaperdirect.co.uk** (except pages 46 to 51, heart design, from a range at Homebase).

Publisher: Beverley Dutton

Editor: Jenny Stewart

Art Director & Designer: Sarah Richardson

Sub Editor: Jenny Royle

Graphic Designer: Zena Manicom

Photography: Alister Thorpe

Printed in China

Thanks

I would like to say a special thank you to the clever girls at Squires, their creativity and flair in putting this book together is greatly appreciated and their endless energy refreshing.

A big thank you to Alister for his fantastic photography, good humour and eye for detail.

A special hug for Elaine, Aysa, Lorraine and Julia for cheering me up when my deadlines loomed and thank you to Mum, Dad, my husband Paul and my children Laura and Shaun for their patience, support, love and understanding.

Thank you also to my daughter's fiancé Michael, for his good humour, easy-going nature and eagerness to help when needed. I really appreciate it.

Contents

Projects

Cake and Filling Recipes

CAKES

Beautifully decorated cakes should taste as good as they look. With careful preparation the following sponge cake recipes are all deliciously moist and light but allow for some simple sculpting if required. If you prefer a heavier cake, I have included recipes for a rich fruit cake and carrot and ginger cake. Once cooled, leave for at least eight hours before cutting layers or sculpting to allow the texture to settle.

The quantities given bake the sponge cakes to a depth of 6-8cm (2½-3"). When the crusts are removed, tops levelled and layers cut, the total height, depending on the depth of the filling, is around 8cm (3"). If you wish to speed up the baking time of sponge cakes and take the worry out of baking evenly throughout, then quantities can be equally split between two tins/pans of the same size. This also means that there is no need to cut layers. The rich fruit cake and carrot and ginger cake recipes both bake to a height of 6-8cm (2½ -3").

Always preheat the oven to the suggested temperature and grease and line the bakeware before preparing the cake mixture. When ready, turn the mixture into the lined bakeware and level the top.

Place in the centre of the oven and bake for the suggested time or until a skewer inserted into the cake comes out clean (see below).

Top Tip

To keep sponge cakes moist whilst baking and to settle the top crust (ensuring the cake bakes level), try placing a flat metal baking sheet/tray on top of the tin; the sheet should overlap the top slightly and sit on the edges. If the mixture rises and sticks to the baking sheet when baked, simply run a palette knife underneath to release.

Check the inside is baked fully by inserting a skewer into the centre; the cake is baked when the skewer is clean when removed. If the skewer is sticky with mixture, place the cake back into the oven and bake further, checking again every 10 minutes. Don't be alarmed if the cake has peaked and looks too deep – cakes, particularly sponge mixes, tend to shrink slightly once cooled.

When baked, remove the cake from the oven and leave to cool in the tin for 10 to 15 minutes. Turn the cake out onto greaseproof paper and wrap carefully. To help keep the cake moist, place the wrapped cake in a large polythene food bag and allow to cool completely.

Sponge cakes have a shelf-life of 7 days; carrot and ginger cake 10 days; and rich fruit cake with the addition of brandy 6 to 12 months, otherwise I recommend no more than 10 days.

♥ Butter Sponge Cake

My butter sponge is a rich, moist and light version of the classic sponge cake that everyone loves. Always use top quality ingredients and your results will be delicious.

Top Tip

A plain sponge cake can be flavoured easily. Try adding lemon zest with a little juice, teaming it with lemon curd and lemon buttercream filling with lemon liqueur sugar syrup. Or try adding a little ground almond and essence to the cake mixture to make a delicious almond cake. Team this with Amaretto flavoured buttercream and sugar syrup, and a marzipan covering (see pages 20 to 22) before the sugarpaste for a fantastic combination.

Recommended fillings:

Vanilla sugar syrup

Seedless raspberry jam and vanilla buttercream

Method:

1. Put the softened butter and caster sugar into a mixer and beat until light and fluffy.

2. Add the eggs one at a time along with a spoonful of the flour and beat well. Add the vanilla essence and then carefully fold in the remaining flour.

3. Bake in a preheated oven at 160°C, 325°F, gas mark 3 until golden brown.

Ingredients Cake size (round/square)

Ingredients	10cm (4")	15cm (6")	20cm (8")	25cm (10")	30cm (12")
Unsalted butter, softened	50g (1¾oz)	150g (5¼oz)	250g (8¾oz)	400g (14oz)	650g (1lb 7oz)
Caster sugar	50g (1¾oz)	150g (5¼oz)	250g (8¾oz)	400g (14oz)	650g (1lb 7oz)
Large eggs	1	3	5	8	13
Self-raising flour, sifted	50g (1¾oz)	150g (5¼oz)	250g (8¾oz)	400g (14oz)	650g (1lb 7oz)
Vanilla essence	2ml (½tsp)	5ml (1tsp)	5-10ml (1-2tsp)	10ml (2tsp)	15ml (1tbsp)
Baking time	40-50 minutes	50 minutes - 1 hour	1-1¼ hours	1¼-1½ hours	1¾-2¼ hours

♥ Chocolate and Orange Swirl Sponge Cake

One of my favourite recipes, this cake combines the richness of dark or milk chocolate against the light butter sponge cake, making a great combination. The addition of orange gives it a wonderful flavour.

Recommended fillings:

Grand Marnier or Cointreau sugar syrup

Orange curd and chocolate ganache

Method:

1. Break the chocolate into a bowl and place over a saucepan filled with hot water (or in a bain-marie). Stir until melted. Allow to cool until slightly warm.

2. Grate the orange zest and squeeze out the juice.

3. Put the softened butter into a mixer along with the light brown sugar and beat at high speed until light and fluffy. Add the eggs one at a time along with a spoonful of the flour and beat well. Carefully fold in the remaining flour. Fold in the cooled chocolate with the orange zest and juice, taking care not to mix.

4. Bake in a preheated oven at 160°C, 325°F, gas mark 3.

Chocolate and Orange Swirl Sponge Cake ingredients table overleaf.

Ingredients   Cake size (round/square)

	10cm (4")	15cm (6")	20cm (8")	25cm (10")	30cm (12")
Unsalted butter, softened	50g (1¾oz)	150g (5¼oz)	250g (8¾oz)	400g (14oz)	650g (1lb 7oz)
Light brown sugar	50g (1¾oz)	150g (5¼oz)	250g (8¾oz)	400g (14oz)	650g (1lb 7oz)
Large eggs	1	3	5	8	13
Self-raising flour, sifted	50g (1¾oz)	150g (5¼oz)	250g (8¾oz)	400g (14oz)	650g (1lb 7oz)
Couverture chocolate (milk or dark)	30g (1oz)	75g (2½oz)	100g (3½oz)	200g (7oz)	300g (10½oz)
Organic orange zest	½ an orange	1 orange	2 oranges	3 oranges	4 oranges
Organic orange juice	10ml (2tsp)	15ml (1tbsp)	30ml (2tbsp)	45ml (3tbsp)	60ml (4tbsp)
Baking time	40-50 minutes	50 minutes - 1 hour	1-1¼ hours	1¼-1½ hours	1¾-2¼ hours

♥ Amaretto Cherry Sponge Cake

Recommended fillings:

Cherry liqueur (Kirsch) sugar syrup

Cherry conserve and vanilla buttercream

Method:

1 Rinse the cherries to remove some of the glacé coating and place on kitchen paper to dry. Chop or slice very thinly.

2 Beat the butter and sugar together until light and fluffy. Add the eggs one at a time with a spoonful of flour and beat until smooth and glossy. Add the Amaretto.

3 Liberally coat the sliced cherries with a little flour; this will prevent them from sinking to the bottom of the cake during baking. Fold remaining flour into the mixture. Gently stir in the cherries.

4 Bake at 160°C, 325°F, gas mark 3.

Amaretto Cherry Sponge Cake ingredients table opposite.

♥ White Chocolate and Lime Sponge Cake

A fabulous alternative to the typical chocolate cake, here's a rich, sumptuous pale cake with an appealing, dense texture. The lime complements the sweetness and richness of the white chocolate perfectly.

Recommended fillings:

Lime juice sugar syrup

White chocolate buttercream

Method:

1 Break the chocolate into a bowl and place over a saucepan filled with hot water (or in a bain-marie). Stir until melted. Allow to cool until slightly warm.

2 Sift the flour and baking powder together in a bowl.

3 Cream the butter and sugar together until light and fluffy. Add the eggs, lime zest and lime juice. Add a third of the flour mixture and stir until combined. Add a third of the buttermilk and stir until combined. Continue alternating one third of each until the ingredients are mixed well. Fold in the cooled, melted chocolate.

4 Bake in a preheated oven at 150°C, 300°F, gas mark 2.

White Chocolate and Lime Sponge Cake ingredients table opposite.

Amaretto Cherry Sponge Cake

Ingredients   Cake size (round/square)

	10cm (4")	15cm (6")	20cm (8")	25cm (10")	30cm (12")
Unsalted butter, softened	50g (1¾oz)	150g (5¼oz)	250g (8¾oz)	400g (14oz)	650g (1lb 7oz)
Caster sugar	50g (1¾oz)	150g (5¼oz)	250g (8¾oz)	400g (14oz)	650g (1lb 7oz)
Large eggs	1	3	5	8	13
Self-raising flour, sifted	50g (1¾oz)	200g (7oz)	300g (10½oz)	450g (1lb)	750g (1lb 10½oz)
Natural colour glacé cherries	50g (1¾oz)	100g (3½oz)	200g (7oz)	350g (12¼oz)	500g (1lb 1¾oz)
Amaretto	10ml (2tsp)	15ml (1tbsp)	30ml (2tbsp)	45ml (3tbsp)	60ml (4tbsp)
Baking time	40-50 minutes	50 minutes - 1 hour	1-1¼ hours	1¼-1½ hours	1¾-2¼ hours

White Chocolate and Lime Sponge Cake

Ingredients   Cake size (round/square)

	10cm (4")	15cm (6")	20cm (8")	25cm (10")	30cm (12")
Plain flour	90g (3oz)	175g (6oz)	350g (12¼oz)	700g (1lb 8¾oz)	1.1kg (2lb 6¾oz)
Baking powder	2ml (½tsp)	5ml (1tsp)	10ml (2tsp)	20ml (4tsp)	30ml (6tsp)
Unsalted butter, softened	45g (1½oz)	75g (2½oz)	150g (5¼oz)	300g (10½oz)	450g (1lb)
Caster sugar	75g (2½oz)	150g (5¼oz)	300g (10½oz)	600g (1lb 5¼oz)	900g (2lb)
Large eggs	1	2	3	6	9
Grated lime zest	5ml (1tsp)	5ml (1tsp)	10ml (2tsp)	20ml (4tsp)	30ml (2tbsp)
Lime juice	10ml (2tsp)	15ml (1tbsp)	15ml (1tbsp)	30ml (2tbsp)	45ml (3tbsp)
Buttermilk	50ml (1¾fl oz)	100ml (3½fl oz)	175ml (6fl oz)	250ml (8¾fl oz)	500ml (17½fl oz)
White chocolate	75g (2½oz)	150g (5¼oz)	300g (10½oz)	500g (1lb 1¾oz)	750g (1lb 10½oz)
Baking time	1¼-1½ hours	1¼-1½ hours	1½-2 hours	1½-2 hours	1¾-2¼ hours

♥ Devil's Food Cake

This chocolate and coffee cake is deliciously moist and dark and has a soft, velvety texture. The coffee adds a subtle smoothness to the taste.

Recommended fillings:

Coffee liqueur (Tia Maria) sugar syrup

Chocolate ganache and seedless raspberry jam

Method:

1 Make the coffee in a heat-resistant bowl. Break the dark chocolate into small pieces and add to the coffee, stirring until melted. Leave to cool.

2 Beat the softened butter and dark brown sugar together until light and fluffy. Gradually add the eggs one at a time, then stir in the vanilla essence and the chocolate and coffee mixture.

3 Sift the plain flour and bicarbonate of soda together and gradually fold into the mixture a little at a time until well blended. Stir in the soured cream.

4 Bake in a preheated oven at 160°C, 325°F, gas mark 3.

Devil's Food Cake ingredients table overleaf.

Ingredients   Cake size (round/square)

	10cm (4")	15cm (6")	20cm (8")	25cm (10")	30cm (12")
Hot, strong black coffee	40ml (1½fl oz)	90ml (3fl oz)	175ml (6fl oz)	350ml (12 1/4oz)	525ml (18½fl oz)
Dark couverture chocolate	20g (¾oz)	45g (2½oz)	75g (2½oz)	150g (5¼oz)	225g (8oz)
Unsalted butter, softened	45g (1½oz)	90g (3oz)	175g (6oz)	350g (12¼oz)	525g (1lb 2¼oz)
Soft dark brown sugar	75g (2½oz)	145g (5oz)	280g (9¾oz)	550g (1lb 3½oz)	820g (1lb 13oz)
Vanilla essence	2ml (½tsp)	5ml (1tsp)	5ml (1tsp)	10ml (2tsp)	15ml (3tsp)
Large eggs	1	2	3	6	9
Plain flour	75g (2½oz)	145g (5oz)	280g (9¾oz)	550g (1lb 3½oz)	820g (1lb 13oz)
Bicarbonate of soda	2ml (½tsp)	5ml (1tsp)	7ml (1½tsp)	15ml (3tsp)	15ml (3tsp)
Soured cream	40ml (1½fl oz)	90ml (3fl oz)	175ml (6fl oz)	350ml (12¼fl oz)	525ml (18½fl oz)
Baking time	45 minutes - 1 hour	1-1¼ hours	1¼-1½ hours	1½-1¾ hours	1¾-2¼ hours

♥ Rich Fruit Cake

This delicious, perfectly honed recipe comes from my Mother and I have to say is one of the best. You may omit the brandy if you prefer although I find it makes the flavour richer. Chopped, softened, dried figs can replace the chopped nuts if required.

This cake is best left to mature for three months from baking, as the flavour becomes richer and the texture firms up for ease of cutting but remains beautifully moist. However, if you are short of time and it is consumed beforehand, it's still absolutely delicious.

Top Tip

Be careful not to over-bake this cake as this burns and dries the fruit and causes a bitter taste.

Recommended coatings:

Apricot glaze

Marzipan

Method:

1   Soak the dried fruit in brandy or sugar syrup. Give the mixture a good stir, place in an airtight container and then leave overnight to soften and become plump.

2   Cream the butter and sugar together until light and fluffy. Add the eggs one at a time, together with a tablespoon of flour.

3   Sift the flour and spice together and then fold into the mixture. Add the black treacle, lemon rind/juice, softened fruit and brandy and stir well.

4   Turn into the prepared bakeware and place on a baking tray. Bake in the centre of a preheated oven at 140°C, 275°F, gas mark 1 until the time stated or when the cake is firm to the touch and a skewer inserted into the centre comes out clean.

5   When the cake is baked, leave to cool completely in the tin. When cold, drizzle brandy to taste over the top of the cake, wrap in greaseproof paper and then double-wrap in cling film (plastic wrap). You can keep adding a little brandy every week to keep it moist and help the cake to mature.

Ingredients   Cake size (round/square)

	10cm (4")	15cm (6")	20cm (8")	25cm (10")	30cm (12")
Currants	20g (¾oz)	75g (2½oz)	125g (4½oz)	280g (9¾oz)	450g (1lb)
Sultanas	50g (1¾oz)	100g (3½oz)	175g (6oz)	375g (13¼oz)	550g (1lb 3½oz)
Raisins	20g (¾oz)	75g (2½oz)	125g (4½oz)	280g (9¾oz)	450g (1lb)
Chopped mixed peel	15g (½oz)	20g (¾oz)	50g (1¾oz)	125g (4½oz)	175g (6oz)
Glacé cherries	20g (¾oz)	50g (1¾oz)	100g (3½oz)	150g (5¼oz)	280g (9¾oz)
Prunes, stoned	20g (¾oz)	50g (1¾oz)	75g (2½oz)	100g (3½oz)	175g (6oz)
Chopped nuts	15g (½oz)	20g (¾oz)	50g (1¾oz)	100g (3½oz)	225g (8oz)
Ground almonds	20g (¾oz)	50g (1¾oz)	75g (2½oz)	100g (3½oz)	175g (6oz)
Unsalted butter, softened	50g (1¾oz)	75g (2½oz)	150g (5¼oz)	350g (12¼oz)	500g (1lb 1¾oz)
Dark soft brown sugar	50g (1¾oz)	75g (2½oz)	150g (5¼oz)	350g (12¼oz)	500g (1lb 1¾oz)
Plain flour	50g (1¾oz)	100g (3½oz)	175g (6oz)	375g (13¼oz)	550g (1lb 3½oz)
Mixed spice	2ml (½tsp)	5ml (1tsp)	5ml (1tsp)	10ml (2tsp)	15ml (1tbsp)
Large eggs	1	2	4	6	10
Organic lemon rind and juice	¼ lemon	½ lemon	1 lemon	1½ lemons	1½ lemons
Black treacle	5ml (1tsp)	10ml (2tsp)	15ml (1tbsp)	15ml (1tbsp)	30ml (2tbsp)
Brandy	10ml (2tsp)	15ml (1tbsp)	30ml (2tbsp)	60ml (4tbsp)	75ml (5tbsp)
Baking time	1½-2 hours	2-2½ hours	3-3½ hours	5-5½ hours	6½-7 hours

♥ Carrot and Ginger Cake

Soft and moist, this cake is a delicious and popular choice at any celebration. As the cake is so dense, I don't usually cut and fill it – a liberal spread of honey over the surface before adding the marzipan and/or sugarpaste complements the cake beautifully. If you prefer not to marzipan the cake and the surface is uneven, a generous coating of white chocolate buttercream not only perfects the shape as it sets firm but complements the flavour of the cake.

Recommended coatings:

Honey (with optional marzipan) or white chocolate buttercream (see note above)

Method:

1 Beat the butter and sugar together until light and fluffy. Add all eggs, vanilla essence and honey, and beat well.

2 Fold in the flour, all dry ingredients, then the carrots and nuts. Stir in the soured cream.

3 Bake in a preheated oven at 150°C, 300°F, gas mark 2.

Carrot and Ginger Cake ingredients table overleaf.

Ingredients   Cake size (round/square)

Ingredients	10cm (4")	15cm (6")	20cm (8")	25cm (10")	30cm (12")
Unsalted butter, softened	50g (1¾oz)	100g (3½oz)	200g (7oz)	400g (14oz)	600g (1lb 5¼oz)
Soft brown sugar	75g (2½oz)	150g (5¼oz)	310g (10¾oz)	625g (1lb 6oz)	925g (2lb¾oz)
Large eggs	1	2	3	6	9
Vanilla extract	5ml (1tsp)	5ml (1tsp)	7ml (1½tsp)	15ml (3tsp)	20ml (4tsp)
Clear honey	10ml (2tsp)	15ml (1tbsp)	30ml (2tbsp)	60ml (4tbsp)	90ml (6tbsp)
Plain, all purpose flour	60g (2oz)	125g (4½oz)	260g (9oz)	525g (1lb 2¼oz)	770g (1lb 11oz)
Bicarbonate of soda	1ml (¼tsp)	2ml (½tsp)	5ml (1tsp)	10ml (2tsp)	15ml (1tbsp)
Baking powder	1ml (¼tsp)	2ml (½tsp)	5ml (1tsp)	10ml (2tsp)	15ml (1tbsp)
Cinnamon	2ml (½tsp)	5ml (1tsp)	10ml (2tsp)	20ml (4tsp)	30ml (2tbsp)
Ginger	7ml (1½tsp)	10ml (2tsp)	15ml (3tsp)	25ml (5tsp)	45ml (3tbsp)
Grated nutmeg (optional)	1ml (¼tsp)	2ml (½tsp)	5ml (1tsp)	10ml (2tsp)	15ml (1tbsp)
Grated carrots	60g (2oz)	125g (4½oz)	260g (9oz)	525g (1lb 2¼oz)	770g (1lb 11oz)
Chopped nuts	20g (¾oz)	50g (1¾oz)	100g (3½oz)	200g (7oz)	300g (10½oz)
Soured cream	15ml (1tbsp)	25ml (¾fl oz)	50ml (1¾fl oz)	100ml (3½fl oz)	150ml (5¼fl oz)
Baking time	1¼-1½ hours	1¼-1¾ hours	1½-2 hours	1¾-2¼ hours	2-2½ hours

Top Tip

If you make wedding cakes as a business, make up a generous quantity of unflavoured sugar syrup, store in the refrigerator (it will keep for up to one month) and flavour the quantity required when needed.

FILLINGS

I have suggested fillings to go with each sponge cake recipe, though you can choose a filling to suit your taste.

♥ Sugar Syrup (Moistening Syrup)

There is demand for a choice of cake flavours for wedding cakes, sometimes in the different tiers of one design – perhaps a rich fruit base, chocolate sponge middle and vanilla sponge top. Rich fruit cake, which contains softened dried fruit and is soaked in brandy, stays beautifully moist. On the other hand, if a sponge cake is exposed to the air the cake can start to dry out almost immediately. To help counteract this problem, sugar syrup can be brushed or dabbed carefully over each sponge cake layer, preferably with a silicone pastry brush and before the cake filling is added. The syrup slowly soaks into the sponge until it is distributed evenly throughout the cake. I also brush syrup over the top and sides of the sponge cake just before the buttercream crumb-coat is spread over the surface as I find it spreads a little easier.

Some cake decorators prefer to be generous when brushing on the syrup whilst others are more conservative – it purely depends on personal choice. I find excessive sugar syrup can cause the sponge to become very sweet, so I recommend the following quantity for a typical 15cm (6"), 20cm (8") and 25cm (10") three-tier wedding cake. You can, of course, add more; in fact, many cake decorators use double these quantities.

Ingredients:
210g (7½oz) sugar

250ml (8¾fl oz) water

5ml (1tsp) flavouring (see cake recipes for suggestions)

Method:

1 Pour the measured sugar into a saucepan along with the water. Heat gently and bring to the boil, stirring carefully. Simmer for one minute to ensure all sugar granules have completely dissolved. Do not leave unattended as sugar can burn easily. Remove from the heat and set aside to cool.

2 Store in an airtight container and refrigerate. Use within one month.

3 Flavouring sugar syrup is not absolutely necessary but if you've baked a flavoured sponge cake then flavouring the sugar syrup to complement it can really enhance the taste. Although the most popular flavouring is vanilla, there is a myriad of choice if you use any of the fruit liqueurs available (a personal favourite is Grand Marnier with orange sponge cake); different seedless fruit jams also work very well. I have suggested different flavourings in the cake recipes (pages 9 to 14).

♥ Buttercream

Makes approximately 625g (1lb 6oz).

Ingredients:
175g (6oz) unsalted butter, softened

30-45ml (2-3tbsp) milk

5ml (1tsp) vanilla essence

450g (1lb) icing sugar, sifted

Method:

1 Place the softened butter, milk and essence into a mixer. Mix on medium speed and add the icing sugar a little at a time. Mix until light, fluffy and pale in colour.

2 Store in an airtight container and use within 10 days. Bring to room temperature and beat again before use.

Basic variations for buttercream:

Chocolate
Fold in 150-200g (5¼-7oz) of melted and cooled dark, milk or white chocolate.

Orange or lemon
Add 30-45ml (2-3 level tbsp) of orange or lemon curd.

Coffee
Add 30-45ml (2-3tbsp) of coffee essence.

Raspberry
Add 30-45ml (2-3 level tbsp) of seedless raspberry jam.

Almond
Add 5ml (1tsp) almond essence.

♥ Ganache

A rich chocolate filling and coating that sets firm, giving a good surface for the sugarpaste covering.

Ingredients:
750g (1lb 10½oz) dark couverture chocolate

750ml (1pt 6½fl oz) fresh whipping cream

Method:

1 Melt the chocolate in a bowl over a pan of hot water (or a bain-marie) to 40°C (105°F).

2 Pour the cream into a saucepan and bring to a simmer for 2-3 minutes. Allow the cream to cool slightly and then whisk the cream into the melted chocolate until combined.

3 Allow the ganache to cool, then transfer into an airtight container and refrigerate. Use within one month.

Basic Equipment

There is a wide variety of equipment available today to help you achieve brilliant results with your cake designs. If you already have sugarcraft tools or you have a good local supplier, please feel free to make the most of the items you have. I am well known for not using much equipment, and I always bear in mind that there may be readers from other countries who may not have the choice that we have here in the UK. I usually only use what is absolutely necessary and specialist equipment that I would highly recommend, items that I use over and over again which are favourites in my small workbox.

Each project gives a comprehensive list of what you will require to decorate the cake, but the items here will give you the basics to get started. A list of recommended suppliers is given on page 112.

♥ Turntable

A turntable allows you to work on the sides of a cake without having to handle it. Make sure the turntable you choose has a good height, i.e. elevates your work to a level that you are comfortable with. Metal turntables are the most sturdy but well-made plastic ones are the most readily available. All turntables can hold a good weight but make sure the one you use keeps the cake level without rocking from side to side.

♥ Small, plain-bladed knife

You will need a small knife to cut and trim ready-to-roll pastes (e.g. sugarpaste and modelling paste). Make sure the handle doesn't impede your movement when cutting.

♥ Rolling pins

Large and small polypropylene rolling pins are a good investment as they are durable and will last for years if looked after well.

♥ Cake smoother

This will help to create a smooth, professional finish when covering cakes and boards with marzipan and sugarpaste.

♥ Sugar shaker

This isn't an absolute necessity as icing sugar could easily be sprinkled by hand, but as it is used frequently when rolling out paste, I would recommend using one. Choose a shaker with generous holes in the lid.

♥ Paintbrushes

I always use good quality artists' paintbrushes as these hold paint and sugar glue well and the hairs do not mark the surface of sugarpaste. I also use brushes to pick up small items so as not to squash them. A range of sizes is available from your local sugarcraft shop – use the round brushes for painting and the flat brushes for dusting.

♥ Cake drums and boards

15mm thick cake drums, often referred to as cake boards, are food safe, lightweight but still strong enough to hold the weight of a heavy cake. The thinner boards (5mm) are still strong and can be used as an alternative or for a design choice.

♥ Cake cards

I use cake cards as separators for tiered cakes. As an alternative (particularly in America), you may find that food-grade foam boards or plastic plates are more readily available. As long as the separator is safe to use with food it does not matter which you choose.

♥ Dowelling rods

These are invaluable as supports for large cakes and can also be used as internal supports for large modelled items. I always use plastic rather than wooden dowels.

♥ Cutters

There are many different cutters available – I tend to use basic flower shapes (blossoms, rose petals and daisies) and simple shapes (such as circles, hearts and squares).

Other useful equipment:

- ♥ Ball tool or bone tool
- ♥ Cake leveller/layer cutter (for sponge cakes only)
- ♥ Cocktail sticks
- ♥ Craft knife
- ♥ Fine scissors
- ♥ Food-grade foam sponge
- ♥ Non-stick board
- ♥ Non-toxic glue stick
- ♥ Palette knives (straight and cranked)
- ♥ Pastry brush
- ♥ Piping bags
- ♥ Piping nozzles (various sizes)
- ♥ Ribbon
- ♥ Ruler
- ♥ Serrated carving knife

Essential Edibles

The edible items you will need are given in a materials list at the beginning of each project. If you are new to cake decorating, it is worth familiarising yourself with the items that you will need to make or purchase before starting on a cake project.

♥ Apricot glaze

This is brushed onto the surface of a rich fruit cake to create a sticky surface for the marzipan. It is ideal for this purpose as it doesn't affect the overall taste of the cake. The simplest way to make apricot glaze is to boil and strain apricot jam and allow to cool before use.

♥ Marzipan

A marzipan covering is applied to rich fruit cakes (after apricot glaze) to seal the cake and give a smooth surface for sugarpaste. If you like the taste, you can use it on sponge cakes as well. Always use a good quality marzipan with a high almond content, such as SK Marzipan.

♥ Cake fillings

Sponge cakes need to be filled and crumb-coated with a filling such as buttercream before being covered with sugarpaste. See page 15 for recipes and flavouring ideas.

♥ Ready-to-roll pastes

Sugarpaste, flower paste (SK Sugar Florist Paste) and modelling paste (SK Mexican Modelling Paste) are

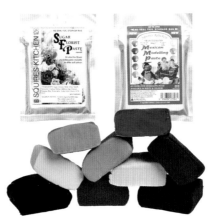

available in a range of ready-made colours. This is ideal if you don't have a range of food colourings to hand, saves time and means that you are guaranteed to have the same colour every time. If you prefer, you can make your own pastes.

♥ Instant mix sugars

Squires Kitchen have developed a range of instant mix sugars which includes royal icing and pastillage – simply add water following the instructions on the pack. If you prefer to make your own, recipes are available from sugarcraft books and websites.

♥ Food colourings

Liquid, paste and dust food colours will allow you to be creative with your work and create your own colour schemes to suit the occasion. Information about how to use colour is given on page 24.

♥ Edible gold and silver paint

This ready-to-use metallic paint from Squires Kitchen can be brushed straight onto sugar work for an instant metallic effect. Alternatively, you can use metallic dust food colours mixed with clear alcohol.

♥ Edible glue

Ready-made edible glue (also known as sugar glue) is available from sugarcraft suppliers. It is easy to use – simply brush a thin coat over the surface of sugarpaste, modelling paste or pastillage and press into place.

♥ Clear alcohol

Clear spirit such as gin, vodka or white rum is brushed onto the surface of a marzipanned cake to help the sugarpaste stick and can also be used to dilute liquid and paste food colours. When mixed with dust food colour it forms a quick-drying, edible paint.

♥ Sugar sticks or raw, dried spaghetti

You can use sugar sticks or strands of raw, dried spaghetti to hold modelled pieces together where extra support is required (see page 25). Sugar sticks are edible but if you use dried spaghetti, I recommend removing it before serving the cake.

Quantity Chart

If the project you are working on requires cakes to be prepared and covered beforehand, you can use this chart as a guide to the amount of filling, marzipan and sugarpaste that will be required. You may also find this information useful if you are making a separate cutting cake or adjusting the number of tiers or the size of a cake.

Filling/covering   Cake size (round/square)

	10cm (4")	15cm (6")	20cm (8")	25cm (10")	30cm (12")
Filling/ crumb coat	150g (5¼oz)	300g (10½oz)	600g (1lb 5¼oz)	1kg (2lb 3¼oz)	1.5kg (3lb 5oz)
Marzipan	500g (1lb 1¾oz)	750g (1lb 10½oz)	1kg (2lb 3¼oz)	1.5kg (3lb 5oz)	2kg (4lb 6½oz)
Sugarpaste	450g (1lb)	700g (1lb 8¾oz)	900g (2lb)	1.3kg (2lb 13¾oz)	1.8kg (3lb 15¼oz)

Covering   Cake drum (board) size (round/square)

	20cm (8")	25cm (10")	30cm (12")	35cm (14")	41cm (16")	46cm (18")	52cm (20")
Sugarpaste	300g (10½oz)	350g (12¼oz)	450g (1lb)	500g (1lb 1¾oz)	750g (1lb 10½oz)	1kg (2lb 3¼oz)	1.3kg (2lb 13¾oz)

Basic Techniques

Most of the projects in this book require the cakes to be prepared beforehand. In the case of a sponge cake, this involves filling and crumb-coating the cake with your chosen filling (see pages 14 to 15). If you are using rich fruit cakes, you will need to apply a coating of marzipan at least 24 hours before covering with sugarpaste to allow the surface to harden, so make sure you allow enough preparation time. Following these basic instructions will give you a level surface on which to work, allowing you to achieve the best possible results when the cake is decorated.

I have also given guidelines for a few other basic cake decorating techniques to help you achieve great results.

 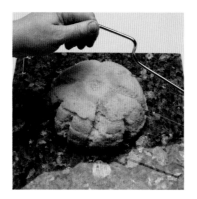 

♥ Preparing a Cake

To prepare a sponge cake for covering with sugarpaste:

1 Trim the crust from the cake and level the top with a cake leveller. Cut 2 to 4 layers in the cake and brush each layer with sugar syrup to keep it moist (see pages 14 to 15). Sandwich the layers together with cake filling, up to 0.5cm (just under ¼") deep.

2 Brush more sugar syrup over the surface of the cake before applying the crumb coat.

3 Using a large palette knife, spread an even layer of cake filling over the surface of the cake. Spread evenly to fill any gaps and create a smooth surface. If crumbs start to appear, add a little more filling and skim over the top surface.

4 Leave the cake to firm or refrigerate until you are ready to cover it with sugarpaste (see page 22). Prior to covering, rework the crumb coat with the palette knife to make it soft enough for the sugarpaste to stick, or brush a little sugar syrup over the surface.

To prepare a rich fruit cake for covering with sugarpaste (using the all-in-one method):

1 As the top of the cake is usually slightly domed, use marzipan to level it off. Brush around the top edge of the cake with a little apricot glaze. Roll a long sausage of marzipan and apply around the top edge of the cake, smoothing it in line with the cake surface to create a neat edge.

2 Turn the cake upside down; the bottom is used as the top

of the cake as it is always flatter and smoother than the top. Position on the cake board (which may need to be covered beforehand, see page 23) or cake card. If there are any holes in the surface, fill them with little pieces of marzipan. Brush the surface of the cake with apricot glaze.

3 Knead the required amount of marzipan (see Quantity Chart on page 19) on a non-stick board dusted with icing sugar. Use a large rolling pin to roughly measure the cake covering area (i.e. across the top and down the sides) and roll out the paste to the required size with a thickness of 3-4mm ($^1/_8$").

4 Lightly sprinkle the top of the marzipan with icing sugar to

Top Tip

Keep rotating the marzipan as you work to create an even shape and to ensure it does not stick to the board.

prevent sticking. To lift the paste, gently place the rolling pin in the centre and lightly fold the paste back over the rolling pin. This will prevent the paste from stretching and tearing. Lift carefully and position over the cake. Smooth the covering down and around the cake with the palm of your hand, pressing gently around the sides to remove any air bubbles.

5 When you have smoothed over the top and sides of the cake, trim away the excess paste from around the base of the cake using a plain-bladed knife. Rub the surface gently with a cake smoother to remove any imperfections and achieve a smooth surface. After smoothing the sides, you may need to re-trim around the base once again to create a neat edge. Leave the marzipan-covered cake to firm for 24 hours.

6 When you are ready to cover the cake with sugarpaste (see below), brush the surface with a little clear alcohol using a pastry brush. This will sterilize the surface and make it damp to help the sugarpaste stick.

To prepare a rich fruit cake for covering with sugarpaste covering the top and sides separately (suitable for tall cakes or where a sharp top edge is required):

1 Repeat steps 1 to 3 above for covering a cake all-in-one. However, instead of rolling out the marzipan big enough to cover the whole cake, roll out a long strip of marzipan and cut to size to match the circumference and depth of the cake.

2 Dust the surface of the marzipan with icing sugar to prevent it from sticking to itself and then roll it into a spiral to help prevent the sugarpaste from stretching out of shape and tearing. Apply the paste around the side of the cake, unrolling it as you work round the cake. Trim the end if necessary and smooth the join closed with your fingertips.

3 There are two ways in which you can cover the top: either roll out the marzipan and cover the top completely and then cut around

the top edge in line with the side covering; or cut a circle the required size (using a cake card or cake tin as a template) from the rolled-out marzipan and place on top of the cake. Gently pinch the join closed around the top edge and use a cake smoother to achieve a smooth, neat surface.

4 Allow to firm for 24 hours and then brush with clear alcohol just before covering with sugarpaste, as above.

♥ Covering a Cake with Sugarpaste

To cover a cake with sugarpaste using the all-in-one method (suitable for most cakes):

1 Knead the required amount of sugarpaste on a non-stick board dusted with icing sugar. Roll out the paste to the required size, lift the paste over the rolling pin and cover the cake in the same way as for the all-in-one marzipan covering (steps 3 to 5).

To cover the top and sides of a cake separately (suitable for tall cakes or where a sharp top edge is required):

1 Follow the same instructions as for the marzipan covering, making sure the join is at the back of the cake. Use a little edible glue if necessary to secure the join.

2 If you need to work on the sugarpaste while it is still soft (e.g. to create the pattern in 60s Love, pages 52 to 57), do this straight away. Otherwise, leave the sugarpaste for several hours as this will give you a firm surface on which to work.

Top Tip

Occasionally, especially when covering unusual cake shapes, you may find you have a stubborn pleat in the sugarpaste. It is often quicker to pinch it together and cut away the spare paste than to stretch it out and smooth it over. To remove the cut line, press the join closed by pinching gently and then rub with your hands until the join is blended in. A little icing sugar on your fingers will help to remove the line completely.

Top Tip

As soon as you take sugarpaste out of its airtight packaging it will start to dry, so always knead it thoroughly and then roll out or shape it as quickly as possible. Re-seal any trimmings in a food-grade polythene bag and keep any spare paste wrapped tightly and stored in an airtight container.

♥ Covering a Cake Board (Drum)

To cover a cake board (drum):

1 Moisten the surface of the cake board slightly with a little cooled, boiled water using a pastry brush.

2 Knead the sugarpaste and roll out on a non-stick board dusted with icing sugar. Make sure the paste is big enough to cover the board and is no more than 2-3mm (just under ⅛") thick.

3 Carefully fold the sugarpaste over the rolling pin, lift the sugarpaste and position it on the cake board. Gently smooth over the top of the covered cake board with a cake smoother.

4 Hold the board underneath with one hand and, using a plain-bladed knife, trim away the excess sugarpaste from around the edge.

5 To finish the board, you will need to trim the edge with co-ordinating 15mm-width ribbon (this is slightly deeper than the cake board to allow for the depth of the sugarpaste covering). Measure the length needed to go around the board and allow an extra 2cm (¾") or so to overlap at the back.

6 Rub a non-toxic, solid glue stick around the cake board edge, taking care not to touch the sugarpaste covering. Starting at the back of the cake, stick the ribbon around the cake board edge, running your finger along the bottom to keep the ribbon straight. Overlap the ribbon slightly and cut off the excess at the join. Ensure the join is positioned at the back of the cake.

♥ Using Colour

Food colourings are available as liquids, pastes and dusts (also known as powders). Liquid colours are generally used for painting onto sugar; pastes are ideal for colouring roll-out icings (such as sugarpaste and modelling paste) and royal icing; and dusts can be brushed onto the surface of sugar pieces or mixed with clear alcohol to make a quick-drying paint.

Squires Kitchen makes a huge range of colours for cake and food decoration. All of their colours are edible, light-fast, tartrazine-free and glycerine-free and are readily available from Squires Kitchen (see page 112) or your local stockist. If you are not using ready-coloured pastes and icings, you will need to colour them at least two hours before starting a project to allow the colour to develop. I would recommend using the following paste food colours from Squires Kitchen's Professional and QFC ranges for the projects in this book:

Black	Black or Blackberry
Blue	
Light	Blue or Gentian
Dark	Wisteria
Brown	
Light	Warm Brown or Teddy Bear Brown
Dark	Dark Brown
Cream	a touch of Berberis
Flesh	Flesh with a touch of Teddy Bear Brown
Green	
Light	equal amounts of Vine and Fern
Dark	Green or Mint
Grey	a touch of Black
Lilac	Lilac
Orange	Orange or Nasturtium
Pink	
Light	Rose
Dark	Fuchsia
Red	Poinsettia
Yellow	
Light	Daffodil
Dark	Sunflower

Top Tip

Paste food colours are concentrated, so only add a tiny amount of colour at a time using a cocktail stick until the desired colour is achieved. Blend the colour into the paste by kneading well and allow to 'rest' in an airtight food-grade polythene bag for a couple of hours.

♥ Dowelling a Cake

If a cake has two or more tiers, you will need to dowel the lower tiers after they have been coated to make sure that the cakes stack evenly and are well-supported and balanced. To dowel a cake:

1 Make a template of the cake top from greaseproof paper and fold in half twice to find the centre. Draw a circle on the paper around the central point – the circle must fit within the size and shape of the tier or separator that will be placed on top in order to support it. Mark the dowel points evenly around the circle – the number of dowels you need will depend on the size of the cake and number of tiers.

2 Using the template and a scriber (or the tip of a knife), mark the position of the dowels on the cake. Insert the plastic dowels into the cake, ensuring that they are vertical and go all the way down to the cake board. Using a pencil, mark each dowel just above the level of the sugarpaste covering, making sure the pencil does not touch the sugarpaste itself.

3 Remove the dowels, place them on a work surface and line up the bottom of each. The markings may vary, so find the mark that is in the middle and score all the dowels at this point with a craft knife (this ensures the cake stands upright and does not lean). Snap each dowel to size and then insert them back into the holes in the cake; they should each sit level with the cake top.

Important Note

Make sure the dowels and any other inedible items on the cake are removed before serving.

♥ Making Sugar Sticks

These are cut or rolled lengths of pastillage and are used as edible supports, mainly to help hold modelled heads in place. If you are short of time, you can use strands of dried, raw spaghetti, but remember to remove them before the figures are eaten.

Makes around 10-20 sugar sticks

Ingredients:

5ml (1 level tsp) royal icing, made to stiff-peak consistency

1.25ml (¼tsp) CMC (SK)

Icing sugar in sugar shaker

Method

1 Knead the CMC into the royal icing until the mixture thickens and forms a paste. If the paste is slightly wet, knead in a little icing sugar until the paste is soft and pliable.

2 Either roll out the paste and cut into different sized strips in various lengths using a plain-bladed knife, or roll individual sausages of paste to the sizes required. Leave to dry, preferably overnight, on a sheet of food-grade foam sponge.

3 Store dried sugar sticks in an airtight container.

CORNWALL COLLEGE
LEARNING CENTRE

♥ Making Mini Wedding Cakes

Mini cakes, cupcakes and cake petit fours are popular at weddings – either alongside a larger cake or instead of one – and look extremely pretty and stylish when presented well. A suggested design is pictured at the end of each project which co-ordinates with the style of the main cake, so you can use this as inspiration or create your own designs.

Mini cakes

Mini cakes can be made in several different shapes, including square, round and heart shapes. Although you can cut these easily from sheet cakes using good quality, deep cutters, I recommend the mini cake bakeware and liners by Squires Kitchen, available from sugarcraft stockists (see page 112). These cake pans are purpose-made which makes the job easier and guarantees the correct shape and size, no matter how many cakes are required.

To cover mini cakes:

1 Crumb-coat the cake with filling or brush with apricot glaze. Roll the sugarpaste (and marzipan if required) a little thinner than you would for a large cake, around 2-3mm (under $^1/_8$") deep, then cover in the usual way (see page 22). Use a cake smoother to press the sides smooth.

2 Trim the paste neatly around the base of the cake. You can speed this up by using a hollow cutter the same shape and slightly larger than the mini cake to cut around the base cleanly and neatly. Simply move the cutter down over the mini cake, press it into the excess paste around the base and then remove.

3 Place each mini cake on a small cake card to protect and seal the cake and then decorate as required.

Cupcakes and petit fours

Cupcakes and cake petit fours can be topped with buttercream, ready-made fondant or a circle of sugarpaste. If the design calls for a little of the cake to show around the edge, brush liberally with sugar syrup so the cake doesn't dry out. I also like to brush a little apricot glaze on the top to help seal it and to make the surface slightly sticky, ready for the covering.

Fortune cookies

Fortune cookies are a novel idea as wedding favours and are a fun talking point with the little personal messages inside. I usually purchase them ready-made and then decorate them to match the wedding cake.

To decorate, dip in royal icing or melted chocolate and then add sugar sprinkles, small cut-out shapes such as hearts, or pipe patterns with royal icing. To add an extra personal touch, you could pipe the name of every guest. Don't decorate them too early as they can soften. Store in an airtight container until you are ready to use them.

Top Tip

Cupcakes, petit fours, cookies and other individual treats are great as wedding favours. Decorate and personalise as required, then place in small boxes or cellophane bags tied with co-ordinating ribbon.

MATERIALS

2 x 25cm (10") square cakes, 8cm (3") depth

2kg (4lb 6½oz) cake filling

Sugarpaste:

    145g (5oz) black; 4kg (8lb 13oz) white

Pastillage: 400g (14oz) white

Modelling paste:

    10g (¼oz) black; 20g (¾oz) brown; 45g (1½oz) dark grey; 10g (¼oz) dark lilac; 25g (just over ¾oz) flesh; 10g (¼oz) lilac; 10g (¼oz) pale grey; 10g (¼oz) pale yellow; 10g (¼oz) pink; 175g (6oz) white

Royal icing: 60g (2oz) white

Icing sugar in a sugar shaker

Edible glue (SK)

3 sugar sticks (see page 25) or raw, dried spaghetti

Dust food colour: green (SK)

Edible gold paint (SK)

EQUIPMENT

40cm (16") round cake board (drum)

24cm x 19cm (9½" x 7½") oblong cake card

Large rolling pin

Cake smoother

Plain-bladed knife

Serrated carving knife

Cake leveller

Palette knife

Plastic food-grade dowelling rods

Pencil

Ruler

Door and bell tower templates (see page 107)

Food-grade foam pad (optional)

Paintbrushes: no. 2 (for glue) and no. 6 (for painting)

Ball or bone tool

Cocktail sticks

Blossom cutter

Piping nozzle: no. 18

2cm (¾") circle cutter

Ribbon: white (to trim cake board)

Non-toxic glue stick

New England Chapel

I've always admired the clean lines of the churches in New England, and with the pretty bell tower makes this design very appealing. The cute couple finish the scene off perfectly.

Note

This project gives instructions on how to make with sponge cake. If you wish to make this cake using a rich fruit base, follow the same instructions on how to carve the cake, assemble the pieces with apricot glaze and cover with a layer of marzipan before applying the sugarpaste coating (see pages 21 to 22).

METHOD

Board

1 Roll out 750g (1lb 10½oz) of white sugarpaste to a thickness of 2-3mm (less than $^1/_8$") and cover the cake board. Polish the surface with a cake smoother to remove any imperfections and achieve a smooth surface and then trim off any excess paste from around the edge. Set aside to dry.

2 Trim the crust from both cakes and level the tops. Trim 5cm (2") from one side of both cakes and put these two strips centrally on top of one of the cakes for the roof. Cut this cake into the roof shape by cutting down either side at an angle to create sloping sides.

3 If using sponge cakes, cut layers in both of the cakes using a cake leveller and fill each layer with your chosen filling. Secure the base cake only onto the cake board with a little cake filling (sponge cakes only). Position the cake slightly off-centre, leaving more room at the front for the bride and groom figures. Crumb-coat the cake by spreading a thin layer of filling over the surface of the cake to help the sugarpaste stick. Place the second cake on the cake card and crumb-coat as before.

4 Roll out 350g (12¼oz) of white sugarpaste and cut out an oblong to cover the top of the cake on the cake board. The cake in this design is double height, so this layer will give the base cake its own sugarpaste coating when cut (see Top Tip on page 48).

5 To ensure the cakes are well supported, they will need to be dowelled (see instructions on page 25). Insert four dowels into the cake on the cake board, positioning them approximately 5cm (2") in from each corner. Mark each dowel level with the sugarpaste, remove, cut to size and insert the dowels back into the holes in the cake so that they are level with the cake top.

6 Place the roof cake on top of the base cake. Use cake filling or marzipan to fill any gaps and to create a smooth surface ready for the sugarpaste covering. Roll out 2kg (4lb 6½oz) of white sugarpaste to a thickness of 3-4mm (1/8") and cut pieces to cover all four vertical sides of the chapel. Use a cake smoother to smooth the surface and remove any imperfections.

7 Roll out 900g (2lb) of sugarpaste and cover the roof completely. Use a cake smoother

to give a perfectly smooth finish. Cut around the shape, leaving the edges slightly proud of the cake. Place a ruler up against the roof on one side and score lines evenly across the paste. Repeat on the opposite side.

8 Cut out the door area at the front of the cake using the template and remove the sugarpaste covering. Cut out three windows on each side and two at the front, each measuring 3cm x 6cm (1¼" x 2¼"). Cut another window centrally above the door measuring 4cm (1½") in height. Thinly roll out some black sugarpaste and cut pieces to fill the spaces in the doorway and windows. Stick in place on the cake.

9 Cover each corner with strips of white modelling paste to disguise the joins and mark with a knife to create a wood effect. Cut strips for the fascia, window sills

and panes, window and door frames. Secure in place with edible glue. Cut strips to decorate the front of the church and to go between the side windows and attach to the walls.

10 Thickly roll out the white sugarpaste trimmings and cut two steps, one deeper than the other. Stick in position at the bottom of the doorway with edible glue.

Bell Tower

11 Roll out the pastillage and cut all the pieces from the templates to make up the bell tower. Cut out three squares, measuring 6.5cm (2½"), 8cm (3") and 9cm (3½"). Roll out and cut twelve middle posts and four slightly thicker end posts, each measuring 4cm (1½") in height. Roll out and cut four rails measuring 8cm (3"). Chamfer the corners so they will fit together neatly. Thinly roll out the pastillage trimmings and cut out the cross for the top of the

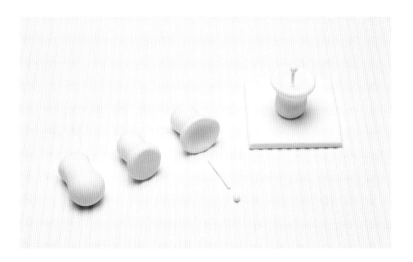

church. Roll four balls for the posts. Set all pieces aside to dry flat, or place on a food-grade foam sheet to speed up drying time.

12 Using 10g (¼oz) of modelling paste, model the bell from a teardrop shape. Push gently into the full end to make a dip and press on the narrow end to round off the point. Stick the bell onto the centre of the 6.5cm (2½") square of pastillage. Push one of the sugar sticks down into the centre and attach a small ball for the bell. Paint the whole bell with edible gold paint.

Doors

13 Roll out some brown modelling paste and use the door template to cut out the door shape. Mark lines with a ruler. Cut strips to decorate the arch and to go across the front and then cut the shape exactly in half to make the two doors. Add two tiny sausages of pale grey modelling paste looped round for handles with a tiny ball on top of each. Set aside to dry.

14 Using the remaining pale grey paste, model several ovals in different sizes for the paving and stick in position in front of the door and steps.

Bride's Dress

15 To make the bottom of the bride's dress, roll 45g (1½oz) of white modelling paste into a teardrop shape. Mark pleats around the sides by pressing in firmly with a paintbrush handle. For the bodice, roll 5g (just under ¼oz) of white paste into a ball and press down gently to flatten slightly. Using a bone or ball tool, press into the top to indent the chest area and then stick in place on top of the dress. Set aside to dry.

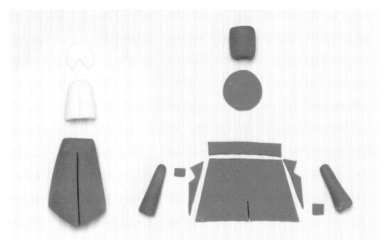

Groom

16 Split 5g (just under ¼oz) of black paste in half and shape into sausage shapes for the shoes. Place each one in the palm of your hand and rock backwards and forwards gently from halfway down to one end to round off the toe area and narrow the centre of each shoe.

17 Roll 20g (¾oz) of dark grey modelling paste into a large teardrop shape. Press down gently to flatten slightly and indent halfway down with a knife to separate the legs. Repeat at the back. Cut each trouser leg at the base to slant slightly and cut off the point of the teardrop, making the waist. Stick on the shoes and then set aside to firm.

18 To make the shirt, roll 5g (just under ¼oz) of white paste into a ball and press down

to flatten slightly. Stick onto the trousers and smooth either side so the shirt sits level with the trousers. Mark a line down the centre. Roll a pea-sized amount into a ball, press flat and cut a small 'v' to make the collar. Stick in place on top of the shirt with edible glue.

19 To make the jacket, thinly roll out 10g (¼oz) of dark grey paste and cut a 5cm (2") square. Make a small cut in the bottom for the flap. Place the figure down onto the strip and cut the sides at an angle from the bottom two corners to narrow the top. Moisten with edible glue and then wrap the jacket around the body, securing at the top. From the trimmings, cut two long triangle shapes for the lapels, cut each to slant at the top and cut out a small 'v' from the side. Roll out and cut large and small squares for pockets, sticking in place and opening

the top of each using the damp glue brush. Mark tiny stitching using the tip of a cocktail stick.

20 Split 5g (just under ¼oz) of dark grey paste in half and roll into two tapered sausage shapes for the sleeves. For the shirt cuffs, roll two small pea-sized balls of white paste and hollow out slightly by pressing in with the end of a paintbrush. Stick onto the bottom of each jacket sleeve then stick the

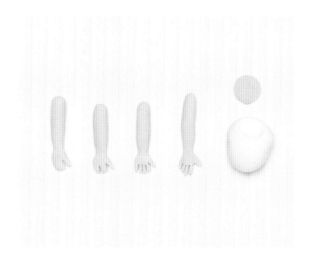

sleeves in place with edible glue. Roll out the grey trimmings and cut a strip measuring 1cm x 4cm (¼ x 1½") for the jacket collar. Wrap around the top of the shoulders and secure at the front with the top corners of each end touching.

Bride

21 Press a small pea-sized piece of flesh tone modelling paste down into the chest area and secure to the bodice with a little edible glue. To make the arms, first split 5g (just under ¼oz) of flesh tone modelling paste into three pieces. Set aside one piece to make the groom's hands later. To make an arm, roll a thin sausage and indent gently at the bottom to round off the hand. Press flat without indenting the paste and then cut no more than halfway down on one side to make the thumb. Make three shorter cuts across the top for fingers. Pull the thumb down out

of the way and smooth the fingers with your fingertip to lengthen them, keeping them slightly parted. Push the thumb down towards the palm from the wrist. For the elbow, press in gently halfway along the arm and pinch out at the back. Repeat for the other arm and then stick the arms in place with edible glue.

22 For the sleeves, roll out some white modelling paste and cut four large blossom shapes. Stick them onto the front and back of each arm and join them at the top. Cut more flowers to edge the base of the dress.

23 Using the reserved flesh paste, make the groom's hands in the same way as they are cut from arms, but using tiny flattened teardrop shapes with the rounded end for the fingers and the point of the teardrop as the wrist.

Heads

24 Split 10g (¼oz) of flesh tone modelling paste in half and roll into ball shapes for the two heads. Flatten each face slightly by rolling gently over the work surface. Indent the smiles by pressing a no. 18 piping nozzle gently into the paste at an upward angle, keeping the smile very close to the chin. Use the tip of a cocktail stick to mark dimples at the corners of the mouth. Push a sugar stick down into each body and push the heads into position, securing at the base with a little edible glue.

25 Roll tiny oval shapes for the noses. Roll two more tiny ovals for the groom's ears and indent the centre of each using the end of the paintbrush. Roll four tiny oval-shaped eyes using black modelling paste. Secure all the features to the heads with a tiny amount of edible glue.

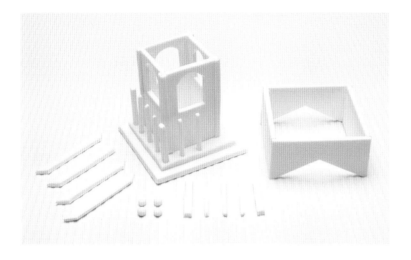

26 Thinly roll out some dark grey paste and cut a circle using the 2cm (¾") circle cutter. Soften the edge slightly by smoothing with your fingertip and then stick in place on top of the groom's head. Roll a sausage using 5g (just under ¼oz) of the dark grey paste, cut both ends flat to make the top of the hat and stick in position. Thinly roll out a little dark lilac paste and cut a strip for the hatband. Secure to the hat with the join at the back.

Hair

27 Thinly roll out the pale yellow modelling paste and cut medium and small blossoms using the cutters. Build up and layer over the bride's head. Make the groom's hair in the same way using the small blossom cutter only.

Accessories

28 For the veil, thinly roll out some white paste and cut a 6cm (2½") square. Cut either side at an angle up to the top, leaving 1cm (³/₈") in the centre. Gently roll the paintbrush handle over the surface to create pleats and then stick in place. Use three petals of a large blossom shape for the tiara.

29 For the groom's bow, roll out the dark lilac paste and cut a thin strip measuring 4cm (1½") in length. Loop over both ends and secure in the centre, then stick in place on the front of the shirt. Stick a tiny strip onto the centre of the bow. Cut two long, tapered ties, trim the ends at an angle and secure in place. Cut two more ribbons of dark lilac and stick onto the front of the bride's dress.

Assembly

30 Following the step picture as a guide, assemble the pieces to build up the bell tower, using white royal icing to stick the pieces together securely. Stick the base of the bell tower onto the surface of the roof, securing with a little edible glue. Stick the 9cm (3½") square of pastillage on top with royal icing. Roll out a little white modelling paste and cut another square measuring 8cm (3"). Stick this in place on top of the 9cm (3½") square. Stick the bell tower housing on the centre. Moisten along the edge of the square and gently push in the posts. Stick the rail on next, securing with royal icing.

31 Turn the bell upside down and secure inside the bell tower housing with royal icing. Stick the roof on top then cut tiny strips to hide the joins. Add tiny balls of modelling paste onto the point and then gently press in the cross.

32 To disguise the join around the base of the bell tower, roll out some white modelling paste and cut strips to go around it. Cut a

Baby blossom cakes

These mini cakes are covered with sugarpaste and decorated simply with flower shapes, giving a stylish appliqué look. Ensure the sugarpaste for the flowers is rolled out thinly, stick the flowers in position so that they are equally spaced and then gently rub around the outside edge of each flower shape to soften the cut edge.

long strip for the length of the roof. Use edible glue to secure the strips in place.

33 Using the remaining lilac and pink paste, cut out all the flowers, indent the centre of each and pinch each petal gently. Stick in place on the bride's dress for the bouquet and attach a pale lilac flower onto the groom's jacket. Model a tiny pink triangular handkerchief for the top pocket.

34 Attach the doors in position using a little edible glue. Dust around the cake with green dust food colour and sprinkle the flowers over the surface. Pipe tiny dots of white royal icing into the centre of each flower to finish.

35 Trim the edge of the cake board with white ribbon, using a non-toxic glue stick to secure it in place.

MATERIALS

Prepared round cakes (filled and crumb-coated or uncovered rich fruit cakes) in following sizes:

> 2 x 20cm (8"), 8cm (3") depth;
> 2 x 15cm (6"), 8cm (3") depth;
> 2 x 10cm (4"), 6cm (2½") depth

5kg (11lb) marzipan (SK) (optional)

30-45ml (2-3tbsp) apricot glaze (only required if using marzipan)

30-45ml (2-3tbsp) clear alcohol (only required if using marzipan)

Sugarpaste: 5kg (11lb) pale cream

Pastillage: 450g (1lb) pale cream

Modelling paste: 45g (1½oz) pale cream

Royal icing: 225g (½lb) pale cream

Icing sugar in a sugar shaker

Edible glue (SK)

A little white vegetable fat

Edible metallic lustre dust colour: gold (SK)

EQUIPMENT

45cm (18") round cake board (drum)

1 x 20cm (8"), 2 x 15cm (6") and 2 x 10cm (4") thin round cake cards or food-grade foam board

Large rolling pin

Cake smoother

Plain-bladed knife

2 or 3 sheets of white card

Scissors

Butterfly cutters (PC)

Non-stick board

Plain piping nozzles: nos. 2, 3, 4, 16 and 18 (PME)

Paintbrushes: no. 2 (for glue) and no. 6 (for dust colour)

Fine stamens: black

Butterfly templates (see page 107)

Plastic food-grade dowelling rods

Pencil

An assortment of flower, blossom, teardrop, heart and circle cutters, all no larger than 3cm (1¼") in length

12 x 30cm (12") lengths of 18-gauge floristry wire: white

Floristry tape: white

Food-grade foam sponge or kitchen paper

Ribbon: cream (to trim cake board)

Non-toxic glue stick

Top Tip

The butterflies are made with pastillage, which can be rolled very thin, dries hard and holds its shape. Once pastillage dries hard, the butterflies can be quite fragile so I recommend that you make a few spare.

Lace Butterflies

This design is so romantic and pretty that I found it difficult to decide on which colour way to choose. Shades of pink would be a beautifully romantic choice, blue and lilac extremely stylish. I decided on elegant shades of cream with a brush of gold for opulence.

METHOD

Board

1 Roll out 1kg (2lb 3¼oz) of pale cream sugarpaste to a depth of 2-3mm (under ⅛") and cover the cake board. Polish the surface with a cake smoother to remove any imperfections and create a smooth surface and then trim away any excess paste from around the edge using a sharp knife. Set aside to dry.

Butterflies

2 To make formers for the butterflies to dry in, cut the card into strips wide enough to support each butterfly and fold in half lengthways. You will need formers to support nineteen butterflies using the large cutter, nine butterflies using the medium and small cutters and ten butterflies cut from the two templates.

Cutter Butterflies

3 To ensure the butterflies can be removed from the cutters easily, rub a little white vegetable fat around the cutting edges. Pastillage crusts over extremely quickly,

so cut out one butterfly at a time and immediately seal any unused paste in a food-grade polythene bag. Thinly roll out a little pastillage on a non-stick board, place the cutter onto the paste and press firmly and evenly. Pull the excess paste away from around the edge of the cutter and then lift up the cutter, leaving the butterfly on the work surface. If the paste stays in the cutter, tease it out gently using the tip of a knife.

4 Using a selection of the different cutters and piping nozzles, cut out different shapes from each butterfly's wings. Whilst the paste is still soft, brush the tips of two fine, black stamens with edible glue and push into the head for the antennae of the butterfly.

5 Place the butterfly into the folded card former. Brush the surface of the paste with a little edible gold dust colour and then leave to dry completely.

Template Butterflies

6 Make the two butterfly templates from card. Thinly roll out some pale cream pastillage on a non-stick board and cut around the shapes, one at a time. Keep the knife blade flat; don't use the tip otherwise the paste will drag and create wrinkles. Roll each wing gently with the rolling pin to thin around the edges. Cut out the shapes from each wing as before and place in the folded card to dry.

7 You will need to make a separate body and head for the template butterflies which will be positioned in the centre. Roll a pea-sized amount of pale cream modelling paste into a long, tapering teardrop shape. Narrow the paste towards the fullest end to create a rounded head. Insert two black stamens into the top of the head as before, then stick the body in position using a little edible glue.

Cakes

8 Position one of the 20cm (8") prepared cakes centrally on the cake board with a little filling underneath to secure it in place. If using marzipan, brush the top of the cake with a little apricot glaze, roll out the marzipan and cover the top of the cake only. Lightly brush the marzipan surface with a little clear alcohol, then cover the cake top with pale cream sugarpaste. If you are not using marzipan, simply place the disc of sugarpaste on top of the cake and use a smoother to create a neat finish. This gives each cake a covering when cut (see Top Tip on page 48 of Cocktail Reception).

Top Tip

Use the cake tin in which the cake was baked as a template for the cake top.

9   To ensure the cakes are well supported, they will need to be dowelled (see instructions on page 25). Insert three dowels into the 20cm (8") cake on the cake board, mark with a pencil, remove, cut to size and re-insert into the cake to that they sit level with the cake top.

10   For the second 20cm (8") round cake, check that the 20cm (8") cake card is the same size as the cake and if not, cut to fit. Using a little filling, attach the cake to the cake card. Place directly on top of the other cake but do not dowel yet. These two cakes will form the bottom tier.

11   Assemble the second and top tier the same way, using cake cards to support the base of each cake. You will need to use three dowels in the base cake only for each tier; the dowels for the top part of the middle tier will be inserted later.

12   If using marzipan, roll out and cover the three double-height cakes one at a time. Cover the top of each cake first, then cut a strip to wrap around the cake side, closing the join at the back and around the top by pinching the paste together gently. Leave the three marzipan-covered cakes to firm for 24 hours.

Note

(Only applies if you are using marzipan.) As each cake is double-height, the top and side of the cakes are covered separately with marzipan rather than in one step as the weight and pressure of the marzipan on the top edge may cause the paste to tear and make the top edge uneven. Using the two-stage method also ensures the top edge of each cake is sharper and neater. The sugarpaste covering is then applied all-in-one.

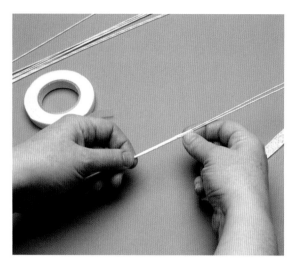

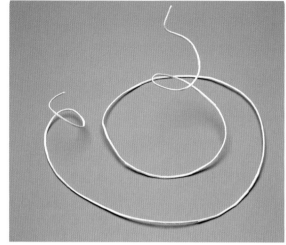

13 To cover the bottom tier with sugarpaste, roll out some pale cream sugarpaste to a thickness of 3-4mm ($^1/_8$"), ensuring the area is large enough for the top and sides of the cake. Cover the base cake completely, stretching out any pleats and smoothing down and around the shape with the palm of your hand. Some sugarpaste brands are more elastic than others, so you may find that you need to cut away some excess paste to avoid tearing. Use a cake smoother to achieve a perfectly smooth surface. Press the cake smoother around the bottom edge to indent a clear cutting line and then trim away any excess paste.

14 Repeat for the middle and the top tier using the remaining pale cream sugarpaste. Once the cakes are covered, dowel the top half of the middle and bottom tiers in the same way as before. (You do not need to dowel the top cake.)

15 Assemble the tiers one on top of the other, securing in place with a little pale cream royal icing. To hide the join around each base, thinly roll out the pale cream sugarpaste trimmings and cut out flowers, circles, dots and hearts using all the assorted cutters and piping nozzles.

Wire Frame

16 To make the wire frame which spirals around the cake supporting all the butterflies, tape the lengths of wire together using white floristry tape. Start at the top with a thickness of two wires, adding more wire as the spiral grows in length until all 12 wire lengths have been used evenly. The total length should be around 200cm (79"). Twist into a spiral and then attach to the cake using a little royal icing.

17 When the royal icing supporting the spiral has

dried completely, attach the butterflies one at a time with royal icing. Hold each one for a few moments until the icing has set and the butterfly is secure. If necessary, use pieces of food-grade foam sponge or rolled up kitchen paper for support whilst drying.

To Finish

18 Randomly dust the cake and butterflies with the edible gold lustre dust using a dry, flat paintbrush.

19 Trim the cake board with cream ribbon.

Mini butterfly cakes

I covered these cakes and boards all-in-one, creating a seamless line out to the board edge. This also saves time are there is no need to trim around the base of the cake. You can use up the small circles cut from the flower shapes to decorate some of the mini cakes, giving a slightly different look to the main cake.

MATERIALS

Rich fruit cakes in the following sizes:
  3 x 13cm (5") diameter spherical (or
  6 x bowl-shaped rich fruit cakes)*
30ml (2tbsp) apricot glaze
1.6kg (3lb 8½oz) marzipan (SK)
15ml (1tbsp) clear alcohol
Sugarpaste:
  300g (10½oz) blue; 300g (10½oz)
  green; 550g (1lb 3½oz) lilac; 840g
  (1lb 13½oz) pink; 550g (1lb 3½oz)
  yellow
Modelling paste:
  595g (1lb 5oz) lilac; 595g (1lb 5oz)
  pink; 595g (1lb 5oz) yellow
Icing sugar in a sugar shaker
Edible glue (SK)

* Use 25cm (10") round/square cake
recipe

EQUIPMENT

3 x 20cm (8") round cake boards
(drums)
Large rolling pin
Cake smoother
Plain-bladed knife
15cm (6") round cake card or template
Paintbrush: no. 2 (for glue)
Food-grade foam sponge
Ribbon: olive, pale blue and peach (to
trim cake boards)
Non-toxic glue stick

Note

For stability, I recommend using rich
fruit cake for this design. If you wish
to serve a sponge cake or you require
more servings, prepare a plain
cutting cake iced with sugarpaste in
one of the rose colours.

Retro Roses

The rose has always been popular as a wedding flower.
This innovative cake uses the classic rose in a stylish
and contemporary design. With big, open petals and an
array of pretty pastel colours, this would
be the perfect choice for a couple
looking for something different.

METHOD

Boards

1 To cover the cake boards
(drums), you will need 300g
(10½oz) each of the pink, blue and
green sugarpaste. Roll out one
colour at a time to a thickness of
2-3mm (under $\frac{1}{8}$") and cover the
cake boards. Polish the surface with
a cake smoother to remove any
imperfections and achieve a smooth
surface and then trim away any
excess paste from around the edge.
Set aside to dry.

Cakes

2 Brush each cake with apricot
glaze. Roll 60g (2oz) of
marzipan into a teardrop shape and
press down onto the top of one of
the spherical cakes, smoothing the
join into the cake surface. Repeat for
the other two cakes.

3 Use the remaining marzipan
to cover each cake. Knead the
marzipan gently and then roll out to
a thickness of 4-5mm (just over $\frac{1}{8}$").
Cover the cake completely, smoothing
down and around the shape, stretching
out any pleats and tucking the excess
marzipan underneath until the whole
cake is evenly covered. If there are
any stubborn pleats, pinch the paste
between your finger and thumb, cut
away the spare paste and press the join
closed.

4 Position the cakes on the
covered cake boards. If you are
short of time you can cover the cakes
with sugarpaste immediately, but I
recommend leaving the marzipan to
firm for 24 hours beforehand.

Petals

5   Each rose is made up of a total of twelve petals as follows:

First layer – one sugarpaste petal

Second layer – two sugarpaste petals interlocked

Third layer – three sugarpaste petals interlocked

Fourth layer – three modelling paste petals interlocked

Fifth layer – three modelling paste petals interlocked

Top Tip

The first few layers of petals are made of sugarpaste whilst the outer petals on the last two layers are made of modelling paste to give them strength. Although modelling paste is edible, it dries quite hard so I would recommend removing these petals before serving.

6   To make a petal, thinly roll out 90g (3oz) of sugarpaste and cut a circle using the 15cm (6") cake card as a template. Reserve the trimmings for further petals. Roll the rolling pin around the outside edge of the circle, pressing firmly to thin and frill the paste, concentrating more around the top edge of the petal. Using the palm of your hand, stroke from the bottom of the petal outwards to the top, indenting faint lines similar to petal veins. Add further lines by gently rolling a paintbrush handle along the paste.

7   Brush the marzipan surface with clear alcohol. Wrap the petal tightly around the rose, covering the marzipan surface completely at the top and making a spiral 1-2cm (½-¾") higher than the top of the marzipan. Don't be concerned if the marzipan around the base is not covered at this stage.

8   Prepare two more petals using sugarpaste. Stick one against the cake, level with the top of the first petal, leaving one end open. Slot the second petal into the opening and close with a little edible glue. Keep the petals tight against the cake and then turn out the top edge of each petal to make them curl round slightly.

9   Prepare three more petals using sugarpaste and attach to the cake, interlocking each petal with the last as before. They should be spaced equally around the cake.

10   Using modelling paste in the same colour as the sugarpaste, repeat this process to make the last two layers with three petals in each layer. To give these petals strength, roll the paste slightly thicker, around 2-3mm (under ⅛"), and only thin the paste around the outside edge. Depending on the consistency of the paste you are

Mini roses

You can use sugarpaste to make all of the petals attached to each mini cake as they are smaller than the main cake so do not need the extra strength of modelling paste. Keep the petals tight around the cake, only turning over the top edge of each to avoid them being damaged when they are handled.

using, you may find it beneficial to allow the modelling paste petals to firm up for a few moments before positioning them on the rose so that they hold their shape. However, do not allow the paste to dry completely, as you will not be able to curl the outer edges over. Support the outer petals with pieces of food-grade foam sponge until completely dry.

To Finish

11 Attach co-ordinating ribbon around the edge of each board using a non-toxic glue stick.

MATERIALS

Prepared round cakes (filled and crumb-coated) in following sizes:

2 x 20cm (8"), 8cm (3") depth; 2 x 15cm (6"), 8cm; (3") depth; 2 x 10cm (4"), 6cm (2½") depth

5kg (11lb) marzipan (SK) (optional)

30-45ml (2-3tbsp) apricot glaze (only required if using marzipan)

30-45ml (2-3tbsp) clear alcohol (only required if using marzipan)

Sugarpaste:

3.5kg (7lb 11oz) blue; 1kg (2lb 3¼oz) white

Pastillage:

145g (5oz) pale blue; 30g (1oz) pink

Modelling paste:

5g (just under ¼oz) black; 5g (just under ¼oz) brown; 5g (just under ¼oz) cream; 30g (1oz) dark grey; 10g (¼oz) flesh; 10g (¼oz) pale grey; 30g (1oz) pale pink; 10g (¼oz) pink; 30g (1oz) white

Royal icing: 30g (1oz) pale blue

Icing sugar in a sugar shaker

Edible glue (SK)

White vegetable fat

Liquid food colour or diluted paste food colour: black (SK)

EQUIPMENT

35cm (14") round cake board (drum)

1 x 20cm (8"), 2 x 15cm (6") and 2 x 10cm (4") thin round cake cards or food-grade foam board

Large rolling pin

Cake smoother

Plain-bladed cutting knife

Figures and heart templates (see pages 108 to 109)

2-3 sheets of white card

Scissors

Food-grade foam pad (optional)

Plastic food-grade dowelling rods

Pencil

Paintbrushes: no. 0 (for painting) and no. 2 (for glue)

Assorted heart cutters, largest 6cm (2½")

Ribbon: cornflower blue (to trim cake board)

Non-toxic glue stick

Cocktail Reception

Depicting the party celebration after the ceremony, here is a beautifully stylish and modern design in soft blue tones, making a striking alternative to the typical wedding cake in white or ivory.

METHOD

Board

1 Roll out 500g (1lb 1¾oz) of blue sugarpaste to a thickness of 2-3mm (under ⅛") and use this to cover the cake board (drum). Polish the surface with a cake smoother to remove any imperfections and achieve a smooth surface. Use a knife to trim away any excess paste from around the edge and set aside to dry.

Silhouette Figures

2 Draw the figures and heart onto thin card. Thinly roll out the blue pastillage and cut out one figure at a time using the templates. Wipe a little white vegetable fat onto the knife and then cut around the shape, using the blade of the knife low against the pastillage to prevent puckering. If you find that the pastillage is drying out too quickly, knead a little white vegetable fat into the paste. Place the figures on a flat surface to dry or use a sheet of food-grade foam to allow the air to circulate underneath and speed up drying time.

Top Tip

Make the silhouette of each figure in advance to allow plenty of drying time

3 Thinly roll out the pink pastillage and cut out two large heart shapes (one spare in case of breakage) and set aside to dry flat.

Cakes

4 Position one of the 20cm (8") prepared cakes centrally on the cake board. If you are using sponge cakes, use a little filling underneath the cake to secure it in place. For rich fruit cakes, brush the top of the cake with a little apricot glaze, roll out a piece of marzipan and cover the top of the cake only. You may find it useful to use the cake tin as a template. Lightly brush the surface of the marzipan with clear alcohol and then cover the top of the cake with blue sugarpaste. If using sponge cake, cover the top of the cake only with a layer of blue sugarpaste.

5 To ensure the cakes are well supported, they will need to

be dowelled (see instructions on page 25). Insert three to five dowels evenly spaced in a circle into the cake on the cake board and mark at the level of the sugarpaste. Remove each dowel, cut to size and re-insert into the cake so that they are level with the cake top.

Top Tip

This method of covering the top of a cake is suitable for all designs where the tiers are double-height (such as the Lace Butterflies design on pages 36 to 41). On serving, the cake is cut from the top down to the board in the centre, and then removed before the base cake is cut. Covering in this way ensures that the base cake on each tier has its own sugarpaste covering on top, so looks professional when served to guests.

6 For the second 20cm (8")
round cake, check that the
20cm (8") cake card is the same size
as the cake and if not, cut to fit. If you
are using sponge cakes, use a little
filling to attach the cake onto the
cake card. Place this cake directly on
top of the first 20cm (8") cake but do
not dowel yet.

7 Put together the second and
top tier the same way, using
cake cards to support the base of
each cake. Dowel the base cakes as
before using three dowels in each;
the dowels for the top part of the
middle tier will be inserted later.

8 If using marzipan, roll out and
cover the three double-height
cakes one at a time. Cover the top
of each cake first, then cut a strip to
wrap around the cake side, closing
the join at the back and around the
top by pinching the paste together
gently. Leave the three marzipan-
covered cakes to firm for 24 hours.

Note

(Only applies if you are using marzipan.)
As each cake is double-height, the
top and side of the cakes are covered
separately with marzipan rather than
in one step as the weight and pressure
of the marzipan on the top edge may
cause the paste to tear and make the
top edge uneven. Using the two-stage
method also ensures the top edge of
each cake is sharper and neater. The
sugarpaste covering is then applied
all-in-one.

9 To cover the bottom tier, roll
out the blue sugarpaste to a
thickness of 3-4mm ($^{1}/_{8}$") and use to
cover the cake completely. Stretch
out any pleats and smooth down and
around the shape with the palm of
your hand. Some sugarpaste brands
are more elastic than others, so you
may find that you need to cut away
some excess paste to avoid tearing.
Use a cake smoother to gain a
perfectly smooth surface. Press the

cake smoother around the bottom edge to indent a clear cutting line and then trim excess away.

10 For each subsequent tier, add white sugarpaste to the remaining blue to lighten the colour slightly and give a subtle effect. The middle tier should be slightly paler than the bottom tier and the top tier lighter still, so add more white after covering the middle tier.

11 Once the cakes are covered, dowel the top half of the middle and bottom tiers in the same way as before, using three and five dowels respectively. (You do not need to dowel the top cake.)

To Finish

12 Dress the dried silhouette figures using the different coloured modelling paste and the templates for guidance. To cover the

areas easily, roll the modelling paste thinly and lay over the silhouette, cutting around the shape carefully with a knife. To avoid air bubbles, only glue the clothing in place after the pieces are cut to shape. Use little dabs of edible glue before smoothing the paste gently. Cut out all the different-sized heart shapes to go around the cake using the remaining pale pink modelling paste.

13 Assemble the tiers one on top of the other, securing with a little royal icing. Stick the figures carefully in position on the cake sides using dabs of royal icing on the back of each figure. Stick the large heart on the top tier, pushing it gently into the sugarpaste covering to secure. Affix the other hearts all over the cake.

14 Paint on the facial features and champagne bubbles using a fine paintbrush and black food colouring. Trim the base board with blue ribbon.

Mini cocktail cakes

To make this design, start by cutting out the hearts to decorate the top of each mini cake and allow to dry. When the mini cakes are freshly covered, press a dried heart shape into the centre, securing with a little edible glue. Press gently but firmly to embed the heart into the covering.

MATERIALS

Prepared round cakes (filled and crumb-coated or marzipan-covered rich fruit cakes) in following sizes:

    30cm (12"), 8cm (3") depth; 20cm (8"), 8cm (3") depth; 15cm (6"), 8cm (3") depth

30-45ml (2-3tbsp) clear alcohol (only required if using marzipan)

Sugarpaste:

    900g (2lb) light green; 2.45kg (5lb 6oz) white

Pastillage: 60g (2oz) light green

Modelling paste:

    tiny piece of black; 15g (½oz) blue; 15g (½oz) brown; 25g (just over ¾oz) flesh; 10g (¼oz) light green; 145g (5oz) light pink; 30g (1oz) orange; 145g (5oz) pink; 115g (4oz) white; 60g (2oz) yellow

Icing sugar in a sugar shaker

Edible glue (SK)

2 sugar sticks (see page 25) or lengths of raw, dried spaghetti

EQUIPMENT

40cm (16") round thin cake board

20cm (8") and 15cm (6") round cake cards

Large and small rolling pins

Plain-bladed knife

Cake smoother

Backdrop and lettering templates (see page 110)

Food-grade foam pad (optional)

Palette knife

Heart, flower, petal and star cutters in various sizes

4cm, 7cm and 9cm (1½", 2¾" and 3½") circle cutters

10cm (4") round, clear acrylic cake separator/stand

Plastic food-grade dowelling rods

Pencil

Paintbrush: no. 2 (for glue)

Plain piping nozzles: nos. 4, 16 and 18 (PME)

Cocktail sticks

Narrow ribbon: pink (to trim cake board)

Non-toxic glue stick

60s Love

I love the funky artwork of the 1960s and was inspired to design a cake inspired by those flower power days. I've included a hippy style couple, dressed in casuals for fun. For a more serious look, this cake looks great just with the circles and love backdrop.

METHOD

Board

1 Roll out 600g (1lb 5¼oz) of white sugarpaste to a thickness of 2-3mm (under 1/8") and cover two thirds of the cake board only. Cut a wavy line along the edge and smooth with your fingers to round off the paste. Roll out 150g (5¼oz) of light green sugarpaste and cover the remaining part of the board, following the wavy line and smoothing the edge as before. Polish the surface with a cake smoother to remove any imperfections and create a smooth surface. Trim away the excess paste from around the edge of the board and set aside to dry.

Pastillage Backdrop

2 Make the backdrop next to allow for drying time. Using the template, thinly roll out the light green pastillage and cut out the shape. If the edge puckers as you cut, lower the knife blade or press gently with the blade to indent the cutting line before you actually cut through. Set the backdrop aside to dry on a flat surface or use a food-grade foam pad to allow air to circulate underneath and speed up drying time.

Cakes

3 Position the largest cake centrally on the cake board with a little filling underneath to secure (the filling is not required if using marzipan-covered rich fruit cakes).

4 Before covering the bottom tier with sugarpaste, rework the crumb coat using a palette knife or add a little more cake filling to the surface to help the sugarpaste stick. For a rich fruit cake, brush the marzipan surface with a little clear alcohol. Knead 1kg (2lb 3¼oz) of white sugarpaste until soft and pliable. Roll to a thickness of 3-4mm (1/8") and use this to cover two thirds of the cake. Stretch out any pleats and smooth down

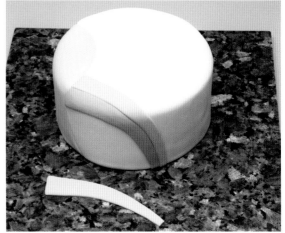

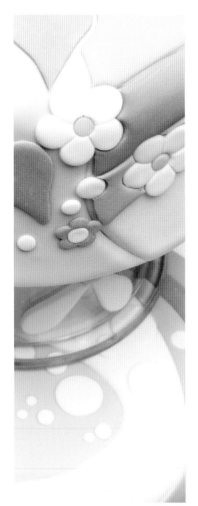

and around the shape with your hands. Cut a wavy line along the edge and smooth as before. Rub the surface with a cake smoother and then trim away any excess paste from around the base. Cover the remaining one third with 500g (1lb 1¾oz) of light green sugarpaste, smooth and trim neatly.

5 Place the two remaining tiers onto cake cards of the same size. If necessary, trim the cards to fit the circumference of each cake and cover with sugarpaste in the same way as before.

Pattern

6 Thinly roll out the pink modelling paste and cut the pink rainbow strips first. Stick in position using a little edible glue. Smooth the surface carefully to remove any air bubbles underneath. Using the cutters, cut out spaces for flowers and petals from the rainbow so the cake surface doesn't become bulky.

7 Thinly roll out the different coloured modelling paste one colour at a time and cut out all the hearts, flowers, stars and polka dots to decorate the cake using the various cutters. Stick the flowers onto the acrylic stand using edible glue.

Dowels

8 To ensure the cakes are well supported and do not lean, they will need to be dowelled (see instructions on page 25). Insert five dowels evenly spaced in a circle into the cake on the cake board and mark at the level of the sugarpaste. Remove each dowel, cut to size and re-insert into the cake so that they are level with the cake top.

9 Carefully position the second tier centrally on top of the bottom tier. Measure carefully and dowel the middle tier with three dowels, keeping them central to support the cake separator.

54

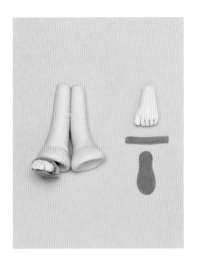

Bride and Groom Figures

10 To make the bride's legs, divide 5g (just under ¼oz) of flesh tone modelling paste in half. Roll one piece into a sausage shape and bend one end round for the foot. Roll the paste gently between your fingers to indent the ankle. Pinch the paste halfway up to shape the knee and press into the back to bend the leg. Use a sharp knife to cut the toes, then smooth and round off the tip of each toe. Mark the toenails by pressing in gently with the end of a paintbrush. Make the second leg and set aside to dry.

11 Take some of the pink, white and orange modelling paste weighing a total of 20g (¾oz) and knead together until streaky. Set aside 5g (just under ¼oz) to make the sleeves later and then roll the remainder into a teardrop shape for the dress and pinch into the full end to indent. Pinch out

an edge around the bottom of the dress. Push the flat tip of a knife into the top to indent her chest area. Stick the dress onto the legs using a little edible glue.

12 Split the remaining streaky paste in half and model the two sleeves. Push the handle of a paintbrush into the end of each sleeve to make a hole ready for the hands to slot into. Stick a pea-sized amount of flesh-coloured paste onto the chest area and mark the cleavage using the tip of a knife.

13 Make the groom's feet following the instructions from the bride's legs, using small pieces of flesh tone modelling paste.

14 Divide the blue modelling paste in half and roll two long teardrop shapes for the trousers. Indent into the full end of each and mark a crease using the paintbrush

handle. Stick the legs together with edible glue and cut the top straight. Reserve the trimmings. Stick the trousers onto the feet.

15 Model the groom's top and sleeves as before using 20g (¾oz) of orange modelling paste and secure in position on top of the trousers. Push a sugar stick or length of dry spaghetti down through each figure, leaving at least 1cm (³/₈") protruding to help hold the heads in place.

16 Moisten the inside of each sleeve on both figures with edible glue and leave to become tacky. To make a hand, roll a pea-sized amount of flesh tone modelling paste into a rounded teardrop shape and press down gently to flatten slightly. Make a cut halfway down on one side for the thumb. Make three more cuts along the top, no further than one third from the top edge, and gently roll each finger to round off the paste.

 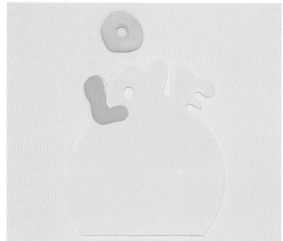

Make the second hand with the thumb on the opposite side. Make hands for both figures and stick in position.

17 To make the heads, split 5g (just under ¼oz) of flesh tone modelling paste in half and roll two ball shapes. Flatten the facial area of each one slightly and push a no. 18 plain piping nozzle into the paste at an upward angle to mark the smiles. Push the tip of a cocktail stick into the corners of each mouth to indent dimples. Roll two tiny round noses and stick to the faces using a tiny amount of edible glue. Take a small piece of black modelling paste and roll two tiny oval-shaped eyes for the bride. Thinly roll out the remaining paste and cut two circles for the groom's sunglasses using the no. 16 plain piping nozzle. Stick the heads in position using a little edible glue.

18 To make the hair, roll the brown modelling paste into thin sausages, flatten slightly and indent down the length using a cocktail stick. Make the beard on the groom slightly thicker at the top. Using the blue trimmings, cut strips for the hair tie on the groom's head. For the bride, twist thin sausages of pink and orange together and attach to the hair.

19 To finish the figures, make a pair of sandals for both. For the groom's soles, roll pea-sized amounts of brown modelling paste into sausages and indent in the centre to narrow slightly. Repeat for the bride using orange paste. Stick them in place on the bottom of each foot using edible glue. Cut strips for the top, making them slightly pointed for the bride, and secure in place.

Assembly

20 When the pastillage backdrop is completely dry, use sausages of pink modelling paste to model the bubble-style lettering. Following the template, stick each letter in position as it is made and smooth gently to close any gaps.

21 To ensure the backdrop is well balanced, build up either side with circles of modelling paste. Roll out the pink modelling paste first and cut two large circles using the 9cm (3½") circle cutter. Smooth around the outside edge to soften and then stick one on each side of the backdrop at the base. Repeat with pale pink using the 7cm (2¾") circle cutter and cut smaller circles of light green for the centre using the 4cm (1½") circle cutter. Moisten along the bottom of the backdrop and stick in place upright on the top tier, pushing down slightly into the sugarpaste covering.

22 Using edible glue, stick the figures in position. Secure narrow pink ribbon around the board edge to finish.

Funky mini cakes

To complement the main cake, I like to make all the mini cakes different. Some are quite involved and similarly decorated to the main cake, whilst others are simple and stylish. To make the marbled design (centre), mix two or more sugarpaste colours until streaky, use this to cover the mini cake and finish the top with a single flower.

MATERIALS

5 prepared cakes (filled and crumb-coated or marzipan-covered rich fruit cakes, except for the 2 round cakes) in following sizes:

25cm (10") square, 8cm (3") depth; 20cm (8") square, 8cm (3") depth; 10cm (4") square, 8cm (3") depth; 2 x 15cm (6") round cakes, 8cm (3") depth

Extra cake filling and sugar syrup (only required if using sponge cake for the top hat)

30-45ml (2-3tbsp) apricot glaze (only required if using marzipan)

1.5kg (3lb 5oz) marzipan (SK) (only required if using rich fruit cake for the top hat)

30-45ml (2-3tbsp) clear alcohol (only required if using marzipan)

Sugarpaste:

1.9kg (4lb 3oz) dark pink; 1.5kg (3lb 5oz) grey; 450g (1lb) pale pink; 1.3kg (2lb 13¾oz) white

Modelling paste:

pea-sized amount of black; 115g (4oz) dark grey; 200g (7oz) dark pink; 90g (3oz) light pink; 260g (9oz) pale grey; 90g (3oz) white

Royal icing: 60g (2oz) white

Icing sugar in a sugar shaker

Edible glue (SK)

Edible silver paint (SK)

30-40 sugar sticks (see page 25) or raw, dried spaghetti

EQUIPMENT

45cm (18") round cake board (drum)

20cm (8") square, 10cm (4") square and 13cm (5") round cake cards or food-grade foam boards

25cm (10") round cake card

Large and small rolling pins

Cake smoother

Small, plain-bladed knife

Palette knife

Plastic food-grade dowelling rods

Pencil

Serrated carving knife

Cake leveller

Paintbrushes: no. 2 (for glue) and no. 1 (for painting)

Piping nozzle: no. 18 (PME) or miniature circle cutter

Ball or bone tool

Clothing templates (see page 110)

Cocktail stick

Petal veiner (any) (SK)

Ribbon: burgundy (to trim cake board) and silver (to decorate parcel)

Non-toxic glue stick

Mouse Party

Beautifully decorated parcels are always popular as a wedding choice, but I had to add these gorgeous mice having wedding celebrations of their own. With or without them, this design would make a beautiful centrepiece at any wedding.

METHOD

Board

1 Roll out 1kg (2lb 3¼oz) of dark pink sugarpaste to a thickness of 2-3mm (under ⅛") and use this to cover the large cake board (drum). Polish the surface with a cake smoother to remove any imperfections and achieve a smooth surface and then trim away any excess paste from around the edge. Cover the 25cm (10") round cake card in the same way using 350g (12¼oz) of grey sugarpaste. Smooth and round off the paste around the sides so the edge of the board cannot be seen. Set both aside to dry.

Cakes

2 Position the largest square cake at an angle on the covered cake board, with one corner at the edge of the cake board to make room for the smaller square later. If you are using sponge cake, spread a little filling underneath to secure the cake in place.

3 Before covering the bottom tier with sugarpaste, rework the crumb coat using

a palette knife or add a little more cake filling to the surface to help the sugarpaste stick. For a rich fruit cake, brush the marzipan surface with a little clear alcohol. Knead 1.3kg (2lb 13¾oz) of white sugarpaste until soft and pliable. Roll to a thickness of 3-4mm (⅛") and use this to cover the base cake completely. Stretch out any pleats and smooth down and around the shape with your hands. Gently rub the surface with a cake smoother and then trim off the excess paste from around the base.

4 Place the two remaining square cakes on their respective cake cards. If necessary, trim the card to fit the shape of the cake. Cover the larger square cake with dark pink sugarpaste and the smaller square with pale pink in the same way as before.

5 To ensure the tiered cakes are well supported, you will need to dowel the two lower tiers (see instructions on page 25). Insert four dowels into the largest cake, ensuring that they are evenly spaced and will not be seen when the next tier is positioned. Mark each dowel level with the top of the cake, remove from the cake and cut to size. Insert the dowels back into the holes in the cake; they should each sit level with the cake top.

6 Dowel the dark pink square cake using three dowels and then position on top of the base tier at a slight angle and secure with a dab of royal icing. Position the small square at the front of the cake board. Using edible silver paint and a no. 1 paintbrush, paint the champagne glasses, hearts and scrolls on the parcels. Wrap silver ribbon around the large, white parcel and secure in place using royal icing.

7 To make the top hat you will need the two round cakes. Trim the crust and level the top of each and then stack one on top of the other. Trim the top in the centre to create a slight dip then trim down the sides to create a slight curve towards the top. Remove the top cake.

8 If you are using sponge cakes, cut them into layers using the cake leveller. Place the top cake onto the cake card (trim to size if necessary) and the base cake in the centre of the covered cake board. Prepare both cakes with cake filling (and sugar syrup if required) and cover the top of the base cake only with a layer of white sugarpaste. For rich fruit cakes, place the top cake onto the cake card (trim to size if necessary), place the base cake in the centre of the covered cake board and brush the top of the base cake with apricot glaze. Cover the top of this cake with marzipan then sugarpaste.

9   Dowel the lower cake (see instructions on page 25). Position the top cake (with cake card) on top of the base so that this tier is double-height. Assembling the cake in this way ensures the lower cake will have its own sugarpaste (and marzipan) covering on top (see Top Tip on page 48).

10   If you are using rich fruit cakes, brush the double-height cake with apricot glaze and cover with marzipan. Cut a disc for the top first, then roll out a strip of marzipan to cover the sides. This ensures the top edge is more defined after covering with sugarpaste. Gently pinch and smooth the joins closed with your fingers and allow to firm. Brush with clear alcohol just before covering with sugarpaste.

11   To cover the top hat, roll out the grey sugarpaste and cover the cake completely, smoothing down and around the shape and stretching out any pleats. Gently rub the surface with a cake smoother and then trim the excess paste from around the edge.

12   For the hatband, thinly roll out the dark grey modelling paste and cut a long strip measuring 3cm (1$\frac{1}{8}$") wide. Stick this in position around the base, securing the join closed and disguising with a dark grey square. Position the top hat on the top of the cake and use a dab of royal icing to secure it in place.

Mice

13   The mice look complicated but are actually quite simple to make. Make a bride and groom, three bridesmaids and three each of the male and female guests. Use 10g (¼oz) of pale grey modelling paste for the head of each adult mouse and 5g (just

under ¼oz) for each of the children, following the instructions below.

14 To make a head, roll a teardrop shape and press a piping nozzle into the paste just below the point to make a mouth. Cut minute squares of white modelling paste for the tiny front teeth and glue in place. For the eyes, indent sockets with the small end of a bone or ball tool, stick a tiny oval of white paste into each and then model oval-shaped black pupils. Add tiny tapering sausages of black paste for the eyelashes.

15 For the ears, model two pea-sized teardrop shapes and indent the centre of each with the bone or ball tool. Stick a tiny, pale pink oval-shaped nose onto the end of the muzzle. When you are ready to position the heads onto each body, push a sugar stick or piece of dry spaghetti into the top of each body and then

gently push the head onto the body, securing with a little edible glue.

16 Each body is a teardrop shape – keep the shape rounded for the male mice; flatten the bottom for the female mice and mark the pleats in their dresses using a paintbrush handle. Use 35g (1¼oz) of modelling paste for the body of each adult male, 45g (1½oz) for the female dresses and 15g (½oz) for each of the children.

17 For the sleeves, roll two small, tapered sausages of modelling paste. Indent and hollow out the narrower end to open up a space for each paw to be held securely. Push a sugar stick into each shoulder to help hold the arms in position before gluing in place.

18 Use the template to make the waistcoats and mark a

line down the centre of each for the join. Use dark grey modelling paste for the back of each waistcoat.

19 To make the shirt front on the groom, roll a small teardrop of white modelling paste, press down to flatten and mark a line down the centre using the back of a knife. Mark tiny buttonholes using the tip of a cocktail stick. Cut the point straight and then stick in place with the rounded end at the bottom and the straight edge at his neck.

20 For the collars, roll pea-sized amounts of modelling paste into ball shapes and press down to flatten. Cut out a small 'v' from one side and then stick the collar in position with the 'v' at the front.

21 For the groom's jacket, thinly roll out some dark grey modelling paste and cut out

the shape using the template. Brush the surface with edible glue then place the groom's body down onto it. Smooth the jacket around the body and turn back the top two corners for the lapels. Make sleeves as before and edge with little white strips for the shirt cuffs.

22 To make the paws, roll two teardrop shapes, press down to flatten slightly and make three cuts along the rounded end. Bend each one over gently and then stick in position. Roll tiny, tapered sausages for the tails, secure to each mouse and then twist and curl each one.

23 For the top hat, flatten a small circle of dark grey paste for the hat rim and stick this on top of the groom's head. Model a teardrop shape for the top of the hat and press each end flat. Re-roll the sides gently to straighten and then stick in place.

24 Cut thin strips of paste for the ties, hatbands and hair ribbons. Cut the end of each strip at a slight angle and secure in place with a little edible glue. For the bride's veil, roll out some white modelling paste and cut a small triangle. Indent pleats by rolling over the surface gently with a paintbrush handle. Use the tip of a cocktail stick to indent along the bottom edge, creating a dotted pattern. Cut the point off at the top to create a straight edge for the top of the bride's head and glue in place. Finish with tiny balls of paste for a tiara.

To Finish

25 Position all the mice on and around the cakes. Thinly roll out some dark pink modelling paste and cut strips for the ribbon on the pale pink parcel. Twist the lengths of ribbon and stick onto the arms of the dancing mice. Paint a silver edge using edible silver paint.

26 To make the confetti, thinly roll out all the pink shades of modelling paste and cut circles using the piping nozzle (or a miniature circle cutter). Press all the confetti shapes into a petal veiner and then sprinkle them around the cake.

27 Secure a length of pink ribbon around the edge of the base board with a non-toxic glue stick.

Mouse mini cakes

Both of these mini cake designs are highly detailed and time consuming to make, using the same techniques as featured on the main cake. I recommend making just a few of each and then mix with a selection of simply covered heart shaped cakes. Scatter tiny sugar petals around them to finish.

MATERIALS

3 prepared cakes (filled and crumb-coated, or marzipan-covered rich fruit cakes) in following shapes and sizes:
   25cm (10") round, 8cm (3") depth
   13cm (5") diameter spherical*
   10cm (4") diameter spherical**
30-45ml (2-3tbsp) clear alcohol (only required if using marzipan)
Pastillage: 175g (6oz) white
Sugarpaste: 3kg (6lb 10oz) white
Modelling paste:
   5g (just under ¼oz) black; 15g (½oz) flesh; 15g (½oz) red; 315g (11oz) white
Royal icing:
   5g (just under ¼oz) brown; 5g (just under ¼oz) cream; 45g (1½oz) white
Icing sugar in a sugar shaker
Edible glue (SK)
2 sugar sticks, 5-10cm (2-4") in length (see page 25) or raw, dried spaghetti
Liquid food colours or diluted paste food colours: black, blue and red (SK)

* Use 20cm (8") cake recipe
** Use 15cm (6") cake recipe

EQUIPMENT

25cm (10") and 40cm (16") round cake boards (drums)
Plain-bladed knife
Plane templates (see page 109)
Large and small rolling pins
4.5cm (1¾") circle cutter
Food-grade foam sponge
Cake smoother
Paintbrushes: no. 2 (for glue); nos. 0 and 2 (for painting)
Ruler
Palette knife
80cm (32") length of 24-gauge floristry wire: silver
Plain piping nozzle: no. 16 (PME)
Parchment paper piping bag
Ribbon: pale blue (to trim cake boards)
Non-toxic glue stick
Cake stand/separator, 23-25cm (9-10") height

Flying High

A fun addition to this humorous but stylish wedding design would be to model some guests hanging onto the bunting, enjoying the ride of course! The bunting could also be personalised with lettering, spelling the names of the happy couple.

METHOD

Plane

1 Roll 285g (10oz) of white modelling paste into a long teardrop shape for the fuselage and cockpit. Narrow the paste at the full end and roll back and forth to create the nose. Pinch the tip up at the back to make the tail, lay the plane body on its side, smooth the tail flat and cut the end straight. The plane should be around 21-22cm (8¼-8½") in length. Using a knife, indent the window area at the front.

Top Tip

To allow plenty of drying time, make the plane fuselage and wings first.

Wings

2 You will need 145g (5oz) of pastillage and the wing template to make the two wings. Make one at a time and keep any remaining paste sealed to prevent the paste from drying out. Roll out the pastillage to a thickness of 1cm (³/₈") and then roll down the

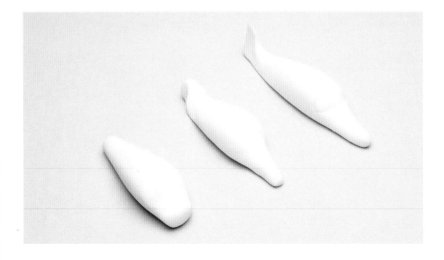

paste again to make it thinner at one end, to a thickness of 5mm (just under ¼"). Cut out the wing shape with the thinner end at the wing tip. Smooth gently along the top surface to round off the slope and mark a line along the top using a knife. Repeat this process for the opposite side, turning the template over.

3 To make the tailplane (small tail wings), roll out some pastillage and cut around the template. To make the turning propeller, thinly roll out some more pastillage and cut a circle using the 4.5cm (1¾") circle cutter. Put all the pieces aside to dry on a flat surface or use a sheet of food-grade foam to allow the air to circulate underneath and speed up drying time.

Boards

4 Roll out 750g (1lb 10½oz) of white sugarpaste to a thickness of 2-3mm (⅛") and cover the large cake board (drum). Polish the surface with a cake smoother to remove any imperfections and achieve a smooth surface. Use a sharp knife to trim away the excess paste from around the edge. Cover the smaller cake board in the same way using 350g (12¼oz) of white sugarpaste.

5 Dilute some blue liquid (or paste) food colouring to a very pale watercolour consistency. Using the large paintbrush, paint streaks across the cake boards for a sky effect and then set both aside to dry.

Cakes

6 Position the largest cake centrally on the 40cm (16") cake board with a little filling underneath to secure (the filling is not required if using marzipan-covered rich fruit cakes).

7 Before covering the cake, rework the crumb coat using a palette knife or add a little more cake filling to the surface to help the sugarpaste stick. For a rich fruit cake, brush the marzipan surface with a little clear alcohol. Knead 1kg (2lb 3¼oz) of white sugarpaste until soft and pliable. Roll to a thickness of 3-4mm (⅛") and use to cover the cake completely, carefully stretching out any pleats and smoothing down and around the shape with your hands. Rub the surface with a cake smoother and then trim away the excess sugarpaste from around the base. Paint a sky effect over the cake in the same way as before.

8 Position the spherical cakes centrally on the smaller cake board, grouped together. Split 315g (11oz) of sugarpaste into three and roll into ball shapes for the smaller clouds. Stick in position against the cakes, two on one side and one on the other. Roll out 750g (1lb 10½oz) of white sugarpaste and cover all the clouds completely, smoothing down and around the shape and trimming away any excess paste from around the base.

9 For the small clouds on the large cake, first split 145g (5oz) of sugarpaste into eight different-sized pieces. Roll into ball shapes and stick together in two groups, one with three and the other five. Knead the remaining white sugarpaste, thinly roll out and cover each group, smoothing down and around the shapes and tucking any excess paste underneath. Position the clouds on the cake and cake board, securing with a little edible glue.

10 Dilute some black liquid (or paste) food colouring and paint the lines on the propeller using a no. 2 paintbrush. Paint the outline of the windows using a fine paintbrush and the template, and then paint a shadow effect on each. Roll out some white modelling paste and cut a strip to edge the bottom of the front window. Secure in place with edible glue.

Bunting

11 Twist the length of wire to make different-sized loops. Close a loop at one end to fit over the tail of the plane and then remove. To make the bunting, thinly roll out red and white modelling paste, cut into 1.5cm (¾") wide strips and then cut into triangles. Brush edible glue along the top of each triangle, fold over the wire and then set aside to dry.

Figures

12 To help hold the figures in position, gently push the sugar sticks (or spaghetti strands) down into the window of the plane at a vertical angle, one slightly higher than the other. Press a pea-sized ball of black modelling paste onto the base of the groom's sugar stick and smooth in line with the surface of the window.

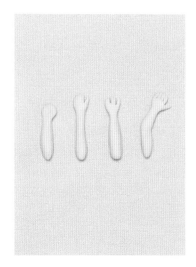

13 Divide 5g (just under ¼oz) of white modelling paste in half and model two teardrop shapes, one for the groom's shirt and the second for the bride's bodice. Stick the groom's shirt in position with the narrow end uppermost and mark a line down the centre. Stick the bodice in position with the fuller end uppermost and make a slight indent in the top ready for her chest.

14 Thinly roll out some black modelling paste and cut a 2cm (¾") square. Brush with edible glue and wrap around the back of the groom for his jacket. To make the sleeves, roll two pea-sized pieces of paste into sausages and indent one end of each using the end of a paintbrush, ready for the hands later. For the hat rim, roll out the paste again and cut a circle using the wide end of a piping nozzle. Model a fat sausage for the top and stick the hat together with a little edible glue. Stick in position at an angle on the

large cake, propped up with a piece of foam sponge for support whilst drying.

15 Roll a pea-sized ball of flesh tone modelling paste and secure into the recess on the bride's bodice. Gently pinch the top to create a neck and mark a cleavage using the tip of a knife. Using two pea-sized pieces of the flesh-coloured paste, make the bride's arms following the step picture as a guide. Stick in position, add a tiny strip of white modelling paste over the top for sleeves and indent pleats using a knife. Split a small pea-sized amount in half and model the groom's hands.

16 Roll two small, ball-shaped heads. Flatten the facial area on both by smoothing gently with your fingertip and indent smiles using the tip of the no. 16 plain piping nozzle. Roll two tiny noses and model ears for the groom,

indenting into the centre of each using the end of a paintbrush. Secure the features in place with edible glue.

17 Thinly roll out the black trimmings and cut a strip for the groom's collar. Thinly roll out the red trimmings and cut a narrow strip for his tie, sticking in position as if it is blowing in the wind.

18 Place the brown royal icing in a piping bag. Cut a small hole in the tip of the bag and pipe the groom's hair. Use a damp paintbrush to arrange the hairstyle. Pipe the bride's hair in the same way using the cream royal icing.

19 Thinly roll out the remaining white modelling paste and cut a strip measuring 5cm (2") in length for the bridal veil. Fold into pleats and stick in position on the bride's head.

Mini flying cakes

For these designs, I covered each cake with a very subtle marbled covering of blue and white sugarpaste to give a light and airy sky effect. This is stylish in itself so you could keep some mini cakes without further decoration to set off the bunting on others. Another variation would be to personalise the bunting with the name of each guest.

20 Paint the eyes and eyebrows with the fine paintbrush and black liquid (or diluted paste) food colouring. Using red food colouring, paint the motif on both sides of the plane and the patterns on the bunting.

To Finish

21 Stick the propeller in position with a dab of royal icing. Model a small teardrop from the trimmings of white modelling paste and stick in position in the centre of the propeller.

22 When the plane is completely dry, stick in position balanced between the two central cake clouds. Make sure the wings line up and are supported by the cake on either side and stick them to the plane using royal icing. Use foam pieces for support whilst drying if necessary.

23 Trim both boards with pale blue ribbon. Place the smaller cake on a separator next to the large cake.

71

MATERIALS

3 sponge or rich fruit cakes in following sizes:

> 25cm (10") square, 6cm (2½") depth; 23cm (9") square, 6cm (2½") depth*; 15cm (6") round 6cm (2½") depth

3.5kg (7lb 11½oz) marzipan (SK) (optional)

30-45ml (2-3tbsp) apricot glaze (only required if using marzipan)

60-90ml (4-6tbsp) clear alcohol (halve this quantity if using sponge cakes)

1.9kg (4lb 3¼oz) cake filling (only required if using sponge cakes)

Sugarpaste:

> 1.9kg (4lb 3¼oz) cream; 1.9kg (4lb 3¼oz) red (with a touch of brown colour added)

Modelling paste:

> 5g (just under ¼oz) black; 225g (½lb) flesh; tiny piece of green; 30g (1oz) red; 10g (¼oz) white; 315g (11oz) yellow

Royal icing: 30g (1oz) white

Icing sugar in a sugar shaker

Edible glue (SK)

Edible metallic paint: gold (SK)

Edible metallic lustre dust colour: gold (SK)

Liquid food colour or diluted paste food colours: black and red (SK)

Paste food colour: white (SK)

Sugar stick (see page 25) or length of raw, dried spaghetti

*Use 20cm (8") square cake recipe.

EQUIPMENT

35cm (14") square cake board (drum)

25cm (10") square cake board or card

25cm (10") square polystyrene cake dummy

20cm (8") and 18cm (7") thin square cake cards or food-grade foam board

10cm (4") thin round cake card or food-grade foam board

Large and small rolling pins

Cake smoother

35cm (14") length of 4cm (1½") width lace

Plain-bladed knife

Sheet of thin card

Paintbrushes: no. 2 (for glue), nos. 00, 2, 6 and 10 (or larger) (for painting)

Serrated carving knife

Cake leveller (if using sponge cakes)

Kitchen paper

Plastic food-grade dowelling rods

Pencil

Plain piping nozzle: no. 1.5 (PME)

Parchment paper piping bag

Pieces of food-grade foam sponge

Template for eyes (see page 107)

Ribbon: gold (to trim cake board)

Non-toxic glue stick

Ganesh's Blessing

〜〜〜〜〜〜〜〜〜〜〜

The Hindu God Ganesh, also known as the Lord of Beginnings and Eliminator of Obstacles, is said to be the most worshipped divinity in India. The way he is portrayed and the items he has around him symbolise many positive attributes and he is honoured at important Hindu ceremonies. This deep spiritual significance makes Ganesh an apt subject for a cake made to celebrate the special union of marriage.

The symbolism of the figure and items around him

- The elephant head denotes divine soul and wisdom
- The human body signifies the earthly existence of human beings
- A goad in upper right hand is used to propel mankind forward and remove obstacles
- A lotus or sprig of the wish-fulfilling tree denotes self-realisation
- The *modak* (sweetened rice ball) symbolises happiness and joy
- The palm signifies blessings
- The broken tusk is a symbol of sacrifice
- His rounded tummy denotes prosperity and the ability to digest good and bad
- Large ears are used to listen more
- The mouse is symbolic in that Ganesh is humble enough to ride the lowest of creatures
- The food at his feet represents material wealth and power

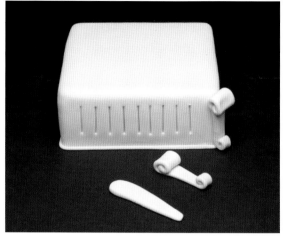

METHOD

Board

1 Roll out 500g (1lb 1¾oz) of red sugarpaste to a thickness of 2-3mm (under ⅛") and cover the cake board (drum). Indent the centre by pressing in with a 25cm (10") square board or card. To make the lace effect embossing, cut a piece of lace at an angle so the corners meet neatly and then position along the edge. Press the lace into the surface of the soft sugarpaste using a cake smoother. Trim off any excess sugarpaste from around the edge and then set aside to dry.

Stand

2 Moisten the square cake dummy with a little edible glue. Roll out 1kg (2lb 3¼oz) of cream sugarpaste and cover the dummy, smoothing down and around the shape. Trim neatly around the base. Smooth the surface with a cake smoother and then stick in position on the centre of the covered cake board. Cut a piece of card measuring 5cm (2") wide, fold over and use the folded edge to indent the vertical lines around the sides. Roll the trimmings into a long, thin sausage of paste and secure this around the bottom edge of the cake. Position any joins at the corners so that they will be hidden.

3 To make the scrolls at the four corners, split 100g (3½oz) of cream sugarpaste into four pieces and roll into long teardrop shapes. Press each one flat using a cake smoother and then moisten with edible glue and roll up gently to create a spiral at either end.

4 Paint the surface of the stand with edible gold paint. As the top will not show, you will only need to paint the sides and just around the top edge. You may need to leave the first coat to dry and paint a second and third coat to build up a good covering. To highlight the lace pattern around the edge of the cake board, brush very lightly over the top surface using a no. 6 paintbrush with only a little gold colouring. Paint dots along the indented line around the dummy.

Note

If you require more servings you can make the gold stand in cake rather than using a dummy. Remember to dowel this cake to support the upper tiers.

Cakes

5 Prepare the cakes by trimming the crust away and levelling the tops. Trim away the top and bottom edge of each cake to obtain the cushion shape. If using sponge cakes, cut layers in each cake with

a cake leveller and sandwich back together with filling. Spread a layer of filling over the surface of each one to seal the cake and to help the sugarpaste stick. If using rich fruit cakes, brush with apricot glaze and cover with marzipan, smoothing over the cushion shapes carefully. Allow to firm, then brush the marzipan with clear alcohol immediately before covering with sugarpaste to make the surface sticky. Position each cake on a cake card 5cm (2") smaller than the cake.

6 To cover the large square cushion, roll out 900g (2lb) of red sugarpaste to a thickness of 3-4mm ($^1/_8$") and cover the cake completely, smoothing down and around the shape and tucking any excess paste underneath. Smooth the surface with a cake smoother. Lift and position on the gold cake stand. For the rope effect around the edge, roll thin sausages of red modelling paste and twist together.

Moisten around the cake with a little edible glue and leave for at least two minutes before positioning the rope in place. (This allows the surface to become sticky enough to hold the rope.)

7 Thinly roll out the red trimmings and cut several narrow strips for the tassels. Using edible glue, stick the tassels in position, building them up at the four corners of the cushion. Roll four oval-shaped tassel ties, indent in the centre of each with the end of a paintbrush and then mark radiating lines from the centre of each. Stick in place to hide the ends of the tassels.

8 Cover the smaller square cushion cake as before using the remaining cream sugarpaste. Mark a seam line around the edge using a knife. Dilute some red liquid (or paste) food colouring to make a pale and translucent colour wash. Moisten the no. 6 paintbrush with

colour and then rub away the excess on kitchen paper to make the brush quite dry. Paint faint lines across the top of the cushion down to the indented line. Paint a line to outline the border and then use a fine brush to paint a filigree pattern.

9 Mix a little edible gold lustre dust with clear alcohol and stipple the colour over the top surface of the large cushion. Brush a little edible gold lustre dust over the smaller cushion using a dry brush.

10 Cover the round cake using the remaining red sugarpaste and indent a line around the sides using a paintbrush handle. Mark pleats with a knife along this indented line. For the piping, roll the red trimmings into a long sausage shape and stick in position with the join at the back.

11 To ensure the cakes are well supported and evenly

CORNWALL COLLEGE
LEARNING CENTRE

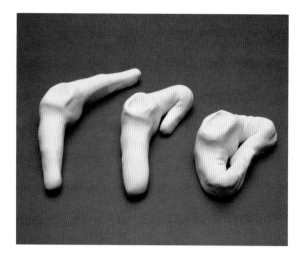

balanced, they will need to be dowelled (see instructions on page 25). Insert four dowels evenly spaced into the large cushion, mark each dowel level with the top of the cake, remove and cut to size. Insert the dowels back into the holes in the cake; they should each sit level with the cake top. Dowel the smaller square cushion in the same way as before. Position the cakes one on top of the other on the gold separator, securing each with a dab of royal icing.

Ganesh

Trousers

12 Roll 285g (10oz) of yellow modelling paste into a sausage shape that is slightly thicker in the centre and bend the two ends round, making the legs. Indent in the centre to make a dip for his body. Pinch the paste at the knee on each leg, push into the back of the knee and bend the legs into position.

Using a damp paintbrush, mark the pleats and folds into the trousers.

Body

13 Roll 75g (2½oz) of flesh modelling paste into a ball. Starting about a third of the way down the paste from the top, indent across the front to shape the chest area and round off his tummy. Pinch gently at the top to make a neck. Roll two tiny circles for the nipples and stick in place on his chest. Stick the body in position onto the trousers. Push a sugar stick down into the neck, leaving 1-2cm (½ -¾") protruding for the head later.

Feet

14 Split 10g (¼oz) of flesh tone modelling paste in half and roll into sausage shapes. Pinch gently at one end to shape each ankle. Cut the big toes and round off, then mark the remaining toes by pressing

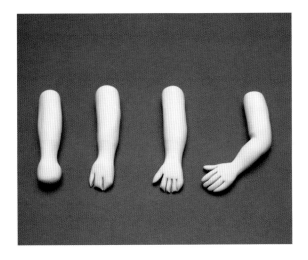

the knife along the front. Stick in position and push gently into the arch of the foot to shape.

Goad

15 Roll a thin sausage of white modelling paste measuring 2.5cm (1") in length for the handle of the goad. To make the blade, roll a small ball, press flat and then use the tip of a piping nozzle to cut out circles from the top and bottom. Stick the blade against the handle and set aside to dry.

Lotus

16 Roll a teardrop from a small piece of red modelling paste and push into the full end with a paintbrush handle. Make five cuts around the edge and open up the flower, then pinch each petal to shape. Stick this onto a small, green calyx made in the same way. To finish, add a thin sausage for a stalk.

Modak (Sweets)

17 For the bowl, roll 5g (just under ¼oz) of flesh tone modelling paste into a ball and press down into the centre to hollow out the paste. For the sweets, roll tiny ball shapes of flesh tone modelling paste and then stipple white paste food colouring over the surface. Place in the bowl.

Arms

18 To model the four arms, split 75g (2½oz) of flesh tone modelling paste into four pieces. To make an arm, roll one piece into a sausage and round off one end for the hand. Press the hand to flatten it slightly and cut the thumb and fingers, using the step picture as a guide. Moisten at the shoulder area with edible glue and then stick the two front arms in position, smoothing gently at each join to blend the paste. Cut the two

remaining arms at each elbow and stick these in position. Support with pieces of foam sponge whilst drying. Stick the items into each hand with edible glue.

19 Thinly roll out some yellow and red modelling paste and cut strips in each colour. Fold each strip gently and drape them around his body, hiding the arm joins at the elbow. Secure in place with a little edible glue.

Head

20 Roll a 45g (1½oz) ball of flesh tone modelling paste and gently pinch out the trunk, rolling it downwards and making a curl at the end. Make holes on either side of the trunk for the tusks. Add tiny tapering sausages over the top of each hole and blend in slightly using a paintbrush. Using the template as a guide, mark the eyes with a

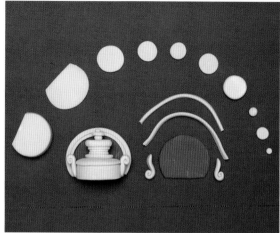

cocktail stick. Cut the top of the head flat, ready for the headpiece. Stick the head in position over the sugar stick. For his tusks, model two tiny teardrop shapes from white modelling paste and cut the tip off one. Stick both tusks in position, securing with a little edible glue.

21 Split 5g (just under ¼oz) of flesh tone modelling paste in half for the two ears. Roll into teardrop shapes and roll a small rolling pin towards the centre of each to indent the paste and create a ridge at the top. Stick in place and add flattened pieces of black modelling paste for hair around the ears, leaving the top of the head uncovered.

22 To make the jewellery, thinly roll out some flesh tone modelling paste and cut strips to decorate his neck, wrists and waist. For the headpiece, thinly roll out some red modelling paste, cut

out a circle using the 4.5cm (1¾") circle cutter and then cut the bottom straight. Using the step picture as a guide, model all the shapes to build up the headpiece. Stick each piece in position then secure the assembled pieces to the head. Add tiny indented circles along the front cut from thinly rolled modelling paste.

23 Place some white royal icing into a piping bag with a no. 1.5 piping nozzle. Pipe all the dots and decoration on the headpiece, jewellery and around his ankles. Pipe a rope effect on the handle of the goad and add decoration around the edges. Allow to dry.

24 Paint the headpiece, jewellery, sweet bowl and edging round the bottom of his trousers gold using edible gold paint. Add tiny balls of red modelling paste in the indented circles on the headpiece.

25 Paint the eyes in the indented lines using black liquid food colour and a fine paintbrush. Paint the detailing down his trunk using red.

Mouse

26 Using a tiny piece of flesh tone modelling paste, make the mouse. Model the body and head from tiny teardrop shapes, then add four paws, two tiny ears and a thin sausage tail. Indent eyes with a cocktail stick. Mix some red modelling paste with a little white and roll a tiny oval-shaped nose.

27 Secure decorative gold ribbon to the edge of the cake board using a non-toxic glue stick.

Mini cushion cakes

Make these sweet cushion-style cakes shallower than normal and keep the rounded top of each cake when baked so that the top edge is soft when covered with sugarpaste. To round off around the base, push the excess sugarpaste covering underneath the cake instead of cutting away neatly.

MATERIALS

2 prepared round cakes
(filled and crumb-coated, or
marzipan-covered rich fruit
cakes) in following sizes:

    30cm (12"), 8cm (3") depth;
    20cm (8"), 8cm (3") depth

30-45ml (2-3tbsp) clear alcohol
(only required if using marzipan)

Sugarpaste: 3kg (6lb 10oz) pink

Modelling paste:

    35g (1¼oz) black; 5g (just
    under ¼oz) brown; 15g (½oz)
    dark grey; 20g (¾oz) dark
    pink; 15g (½oz) flesh; 15g
    (½oz) pale blue; 15g (½oz)
    pale green; 5g (just under
    ¼oz) pale yellow; 650g (1lb
    7oz) white

Royal icing: 20g (¾oz) pink

Icing sugar in a sugar shaker

Edible glue (SK)

2 sugar sticks (see page 25) or
raw dried spaghetti

Liquid food colour or diluted
paste food colour: black (SK)

Dust food colour: pink (SK)

Edible metallic lustre dust
colours: silver and sparkle (SK)

Edible glitter: clear or silver

EQUIPMENT

40cm (16") round cake board
(drum)

20cm (8") thin round cake card
or food-grade foam board

Large and small rolling pins

Cake smoother

Plain-bladed knife

Palette knife

Plastic food-grade dowelling
rods

Pencil

Bonnet template (see page 108)

Sheet of white card

Ruler

0.5cm (¼") and 2cm (¾") circle
cutters

Paintbrushes: no. 2 (for glue),
no. 0 (for painting)

Piping nozzles: nos. 0 and 16
(PME)

Cocktail stick

Silver embroidery thread

Blossom plunger cutter

Miniature heart cutter

Narrow heart ribbon: pink (to
trim cake)

Ribbon: pink (to trim cake
board)

Non-toxic glue stick

Beetle Love

Our love affair with the VW Beetle
goes on and on and is synonymous
with being young and carefree, so is
perfect for any young – or young at
heart – couple. I designed the cake
to be simple and stylish, to keep the
emphasis on the car that can be
removed and kept as a memento of
the special day.

METHOD

Board

1. Roll out 750g (1lb 10½oz) of pink sugarpaste to
a thickness of 2-3mm (under ⅛") and use this to
cover the cake board (drum). Polish the surface with
a cake smoother to remove any imperfections and
achieve a smooth surface and then trim off any excess
from around the edge. Set aside to dry.

Cakes

2. Position the largest cake centrally on the cake
board with a little filling underneath to secure
(the filling is not required if using marzipan-covered rich
fruit cakes).

3. To cover the bottom tier with sugarpaste, rework
the crumb coat with a palette knife or add a little
more cake filling to the surface to help the sugarpaste
stick. If you are using rich fruit cakes, brush the marzipan
surface with a little clear alcohol. Knead 1.5kg (3lb 5oz)
of pink sugarpaste until soft and pliable. Roll to

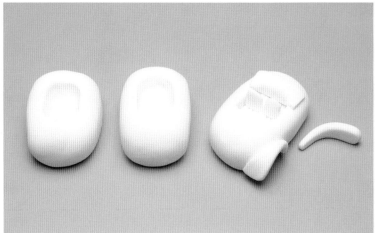

a thickness of 3-4mm (⅛") and use this to cover the base cake completely. Stretch out any pleats and smooth down and around the shape with your hands. Gently rub the surface with a cake smoother to create a neat finish and then trim away the excess paste from around the base.

4 Place the remaining cake on the cake card of the same size and, if necessary, trim the card to fit the circumference of the cake. Cover the cake with pink sugarpaste in the same way as before.

5 To ensure the cakes are well supported, you will need to dowel the bottom tier (see instructions on page 25). Insert five dowels into the cake, evenly spaced in a circle, mark with a pencil, remove and cut to size. Insert the dowels back into the holes in the cake so that they are level with the cake top.

VW Beetle

6 To obtain the basic shape of the car, roll 500g (1lb 1¾oz) of white modelling paste into a fat, rounded sausage shape. Press into the centre to open up the inside seating area using the end of a large rolling pin and then cut the sides to straighten. The paste will still sink slightly, so as the car dries, keep pressing it back into shape. Lay the car on its side for a few minutes and then turn it over and do the same to straighten the opposite side.

7 Make the frame for the windscreen next to allow for drying time. Roll out some white modelling paste and cut a rectangle measuring 3cm x 6cm (1¼" x 2⅜"). Cut out the windscreen from the centre, leaving the frame around the top edge. Using the rectangle cut from the centre, smooth around the edge to soften the shape and

stick this in position behind the seats for the soft top.

8 Indent one side of the bonnet by pressing the template down into it and then turn it over and repeat on the opposite side. Mark the doors with a knife. Thinly roll out some white modelling paste and cut a square slightly smaller than the floor inside the car. Indent even lines using a ruler and then stick in position. Roll a sausage using 5g (just under ¼oz) of white paste, press down and cut in half to make the two seat backs. Stick in position in the middle of the floor with edible glue.

Wheels

9 Split 30g (1oz) of black modelling paste into four pieces. Roll each piece into a ball and press down to flatten slightly using the cake smoother. Press the 0.5cm (¼") and 2cm (¾") circle

cutters into the centre of each and then indent using the end of a paintbrush. Whilst the wheels are still soft, smooth a little edible silver lustre dust onto the surface using your fingertip. Stick each wheel in position on the car.

10 To make the steering wheel, roll out some black modelling paste and cut a circle using the 2cm (¾") circle cutter. Cut out circles around the edge using the no. 16 piping nozzle. Stick in position and add a small circle from the piping nozzle on the centre.

11 To make the wheel arches, split 60g (2oz) of white modelling paste into four. Model each piece into a teardrop shape, flatten slightly by pressing down with the cake smoother and stick over each wheel with edible glue.

12 Roll sausage shapes for the bumpers and add

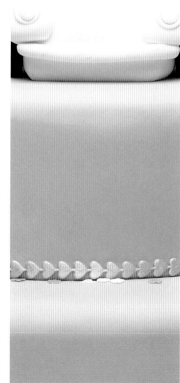

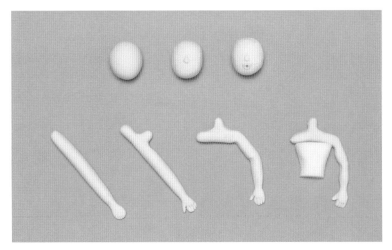

smaller sausage-shaped supports. Secure to the front and back of the car with edible glue. Roll small ball shapes for the headlights, press flat and indent a circle in the centre using the smaller circle cutter. Secure in place. Add two pea-sized amounts for the side windows and roll two tiny strips for door handles. Roll out and cut a strip for the bottom of the windscreen and two strips for the running boards.

13 For the boot, cut a small triangular door and soften the corners by smoothing the paste gently. Stick in position with a semi circle cut from the larger circle cutter and a small rectangle for the 'Just Married' sign. Mark tiny vents along the top, just below the soft top, using the tip of a knife. For the back lights, stick two pea-sized ball shapes onto the back wheel arches, indent in the centre and fill with a ball of pink paste.

Bride

14 To make the skirt, stick a small, flattened piece of white modelling paste onto the front seat and smooth down. For her bodice, roll 5g (just under ¼oz) of white paste into a teardrop shape and cut the top and bottom straight. Using the step picture as a guide, model her chest and arm piece using 5g (just under ¼oz) of flesh tone modelling paste. Stick both pieces in position in the car using a little edible glue.

Groom

15 To make the groom's jacket, roll 10g (¼oz) of dark grey modelling paste into an oval shape and press down to flatten slightly. Make a cut down either side for the sleeves and pinch down to lengthen and round off the arms. Press into the neck area with the flat of a knife to indent the paste. Bend

each sleeve halfway down and stick the jacket into the seat with one arm around the bride. Thinly roll out a small piece of the dark grey paste and cut a strip for the jacket collar.

16 Model a pea-sized teardrop shape from white modelling paste and stick onto the front of the groom's jacket for his shirt. Model a tiny pink teardrop-shaped tie. Stick two tiny flattened ball shapes onto the end of each sleeve for cuffs and indent into the centre of each to make a hole ready for the hands later. Push a sugar stick down through the top of both figures ready to help hold the heads in position.

Heads

17 To make their heads, split 5g (just under ¼oz) of flesh tone modelling paste in half and roll each half into a ball. Smooth one side flat for the facial area. Model

two tiny triangular noses and stick in position, just below the centre. For the kissing lips, model two tiny triangular shapes, stick in position and mark lines across each to separate the top and bottom lips. Indent the centre of each with the tip of a cocktail stick.

18 For the groom, model two tiny oval-shaped ears, secure in place and indent the centre of each with the end of a paintbrush. Paint the eyes and eyebrows using a fine paintbrush and black food colouring. Brush a little pink dust food colour onto their cheeks. Stick the heads in position facing each other. Paint the wording 'Just Married' onto the back of the car.

Hands

19 To make the groom's hands, roll two pea-sized amounts of flesh tone modelling

paste into teardrop shapes and press to flatten slightly. Make cuts for the thumbs on opposite sides and then shorter cuts for the fingers across the top. Gently round off the edges and squeeze the fingers together. Stick in position with a little edible glue.

Hair

20 For the bride's hair, roll a long sausage of pale yellow modelling paste and press flat. Moisten her head with edible glue and spiral the paste around, starting at the back of her head. Pinch up the end to create a quiff at the front. For the groom, shape a flattened circle from half of the brown modelling paste and stick this onto his head. Gently pinch and pull down the paste by his ears for sideburns.

21 To make the veil, thinly roll out some white modelling paste and cut out a triangle. Indent

the surface with the handle of a paintbrush and cut small circles for the pattern using the small piping nozzle. Stick the veil in position on the bride's hair. To make the pink rose, roll a tiny flattened sausage of paste into a spiral and secure to the veil.

22 Position the car on the top tier and secure in place with a little edible glue.

Cans, Envelope and Boot

23 Using the various colours of modelling paste, model sausage shapes and cut straight at either end to make the cans. Mark the top of each using the small circle cutter and make a hole with a cocktail stick. Decorate with heart shapes. For the envelope, cut a small oblong and indent using a knife. For the boot, roll the remaining brown paste into a sausage shape, bend and pinch up the toe area and round

it off. Mark the sole with a knife. Pinch at the top to open slightly.

24 Cut the embroidery thread into six lengths measuring around 8cm (3") each. Moisten the area where the thread will be inserted with a little edible glue and then push the embroidery thread into the paste using a cocktail stick. Tie the opposite end around the bumper. Secure the modelled pieces in position with a little edible glue.

To Finish

25 Using the coloured modelling paste, make the confetti by thinly rolling out the paste and cutting flower, heart and horseshoe shapes. For the horseshoe shape, cut tiny strips, bend round and mark with a cocktail stick.

26 Make two small holes in the top of the car ready for the windscreen and then carefully slot it into position. Mix some silver metallic lustre dust with cooled, boiled water and paint silver lines over the bumpers, wing mirrors and windscreen.

27 Put a dab of pink royal icing in the centre of the larger cake and carefully position the top tier in place. Attach the pink heart ribbon around the base of each cake with a little royal icing. Attach pink ribbon around the edge of the cake board with a non-toxic glue stick.

28 Sprinkle the sugar confetti, sparkle dust and edible glitter around the base of each cake.

'Just married' mini cakes

As the main cake is simply decorated, I have kept the mini cakes the same – some have a sprinkling of small cut-out shapes, some have a sprinkling here and there of edible glitter to give a pretty sparkle. A quick wrap of silver thread on a few will give a different look and is easily removed before being consumed.

MATERIALS

3 prepared round cakes (filled and crumb-coated, or marzipan-covered rich fruit cakes) in following sizes:

25cm (10"), 8cm (3") depth
20cm (8"), 8cm (3") depth
15cm (6"), 8cm (3") depth
10cm (4"), 8cm (3") depth

30-45ml (2-3tbsp) clear alcohol (only required if using marzipan)

Sugarpaste: 3.66kg (8lb 1oz) white

Modelling paste: 60g (2oz) white

Royal icing:
200g (7oz) black
30g (1oz) white

Pastillage: 10g (¼oz) white

Icing sugar in a sugar shaker

Edible glue (SK)

Liquid food colour or diluted paste food colour: black (SK)

Confectioners' glaze (SK) (optional)

EQUIPMENT

35cm (14") and 20cm (8") round cake boards (drums)

20cm (8"), 15cm (6") and 10cm (4") round cake cards, thin boards or food-grade foam boards

Large and small rolling pins

Cake smoother

Plain-bladed knife

Violin and wording templates (see pages 110 to 111)

Sheet of white card

Paintbrushes: no. 2 (for glue) and no. 4 (for painting)

Food-grade foam pad (optional)

Non-stick board

Non-stick waxed paper, cellophane or parchment paper (for piping royal icing)

Plain piping nozzles: nos. 1.5, 3 and 4 (PME)

Masking tape

Cranked and straight palette knives

Floristry tape: green

18- and 24-gauge floristry wire: green

Plastic food-grade dowelling rods

Pencil

Cake separator

Parchment paper piping bags

Ribbon: white (to trim cake board)

Non-toxic glue stick

Top Tip

Make the violin pieces well in advance to allow plenty of drying time

Wedding March

The popular song that accompanies the bride as she walks down the aisle inspired this romantic design. The clean, contrasting black and white lines and the graceful musical notes make a very stylish and striking wedding cake.

METHOD

Board

1 Roll out 500g (1lb 1¾oz) of white sugarpaste to a thickness of 2-3mm (under ⅛") and cover the large cake board (drum). Polish the surface with a cake smoother to remove any imperfections and achieve a smooth surface. Using a sharp knife, trim away the excess paste from around the edge. Cover the smaller cake board in the same way using 300g (10½oz) of white sugarpaste. Thinly roll out 260g (9oz) of white sugarpaste and cover the 15cm (6") cake card. Set all three aside to dry.

Violin

2 Make the templates for all the violin pieces from card. Thinly roll out some white modelling paste and cut out the back piece. Cut out another shape using the same template for the front piece. Cut a third piece the same and then cut out the 'f' holes on either side. Thinly roll out the trimmings and cut a long strip measuring 1cm (¼") wide. Brush one long edge with edible glue and stick in position around the edge of the back piece of the violin. Roll the pastillage into a strip

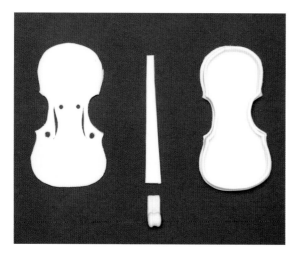

and cut out the piece for the neck using the template. Set all pieces aside to dry on a flat surface or a piece of food-grade foam sponge.

Words and Musical Notes

3 Tape the templates for the wording onto a spare board and then secure a sheet of waxed paper or parchment paper over the top. Place some black-coloured royal icing into a piping bag fitted with a no. 3 piping nozzle and pipe the wording onto the paper. Use the same method to pipe the musical notes, this time with a no. 4 nozzle. Set the piped pieces aside to dry for a few hours.

4 When the piping is completely dry, carefully release the wording and notes from the paper by sliding a cranked palette knife underneath them.

Wire Frame

5 Stretch the floristry tape to release the glue and then twist around the lengths of wire, keeping the tape tight to keep the surface smooth. Twist the narrower, 24-gauge wire to group the 18-gauge wires in sets of five with the ends uneven. Make three frames and twist one round for the top tier. Paint the taped wires with black liquid (or diluted paste) food colouring.

Top Tip

The colouring on the floristry tape remains tacky so can discolour the cake if left for more than a few hours. To prevent this, brush the surface after painting with a little confectioners' glaze or use a little edible glue.

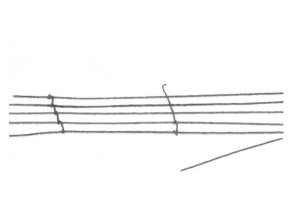

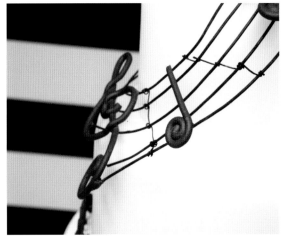

Cakes

6 Position the largest cake centrally on the cake board with a little filling underneath to secure (the filling is not required if using marzipan-covered rich fruit cakes).

7 Before covering the bottom tier with sugarpaste, rework the crumb coat using a palette knife or add a little more cake filling to the surface to help the sugarpaste stick. For a rich fruit cake, brush the marzipan surface with a little clear alcohol. Knead 1kg (2lb 3¼oz) of white sugarpaste until soft and pliable. Roll to a thickness of 3-4mm (⅛") and use this to cover the base cake completely. Stretch out any pleats and smooth the paste across the top and down the sides. Rub the surface with a cake smoother to create a neat finish and then trim away the excess sugarpaste from around the base.

8 Place the 10cm (4") and 20cm (8") cakes onto cake cards of the same size – you may need to trim the cards to fit the circumference if necessary. Place the 15cm (6") cake in the centre of the 20cm (8") cake board. Cover all the cakes with white sugarpaste in the same way as before.

9 To ensure the cakes are well supported, you will need to dowel the three lower tiers (see instructions on page 25). Insert five dowels, evenly spaced in a circle, into the largest cake, mark with a pencil, remove and cut to size. Insert the dowels back into the holes in the cake so that they are level with the cake top.

10 Carefully position the second tier in place centrally on top of the bottom tier. Dowel the second tier using three dowels, keeping the dowels central. Use a dab of royal icing to secure the

covered 15cm (6") cake card on top. This will support the cake separator. Dowel the 15cm (6") cake and place the 10cm (4") cake on top.

Assembly

11 When the violin pieces are dry, stick them together with white royal icing. Using white modelling paste, model the scroll and pegs at the top of the violin. For the scroll, roll a small sausage of paste and indent in the centre. Moisten with edible glue and then roll up. Make four tiny pegs and glue in place. Attach to the top of the pastillage neck.

12 Using the no. 1.5 piping nozzle and white royal icing, pipe all the details onto the violin, including outlining the top of the violin and the strings.

13 Attach the wire frame for the top tier and carefully

put the violin in the centre. Support the violin with some of the wires at the back and secure in place with a dab of royal icing. Attach the remaining two wire frames to the bottom two tiers. Stick all the musical notes and lettering in position, using small spots of royal icing to secure.

14 Secure ribbon to the edge of each board using a non-toxic glue stick.

Musical mini cakes

These two-tiered mini cakes are extremely eye-catching when placed on the table for each guest. To obtain the shape and look, you will need to cut each round mini cake in half horizontally and then cut a smaller cake from one half using a circle cutter. The wording is piped directly onto the cake surface when the sugarpaste covering has firmed. You can team these tiered cakes with quick and easy cupcakes decorated with black or white filigree lace effect on the top. For a splash of colour, add a red or bright pink heart to the centre.

MATERIALS

2 cakes in following sizes:

25cm (10") round, 8cm (3") depth (filled and crumb-coated, or marzipan-covered rich fruit cake)

15cm (6") bowl-shaped sponge cake, 8cm (3") depth*

315g (11oz) cake filling (only required if using sponge cakes)

450g (1lb) marzipan (SK) (optional)

30-45ml (2-3tbsp) clear alcohol (only required if using marzipan)

Sugarpaste: 3kg (6lb 10oz) white

Modelling paste:

5g (just under ¼oz) black; 115g (4oz) dark grey; 30g (1oz) flesh ; 10g (¼oz) pale grey; 595g (1lb 5oz) white

Royal icing:

10g (¼oz) brown; 10g (¼oz) light brown; 10g (¼oz) pale green; 45g (1½oz) white

Icing sugar in a sugar shaker

Edible glue (SK)

2 sugar sticks, 5cm (2") in length (see page 25) or raw, dried spaghetti

Liquid food colours: black and red (SK)

Dust food colour: pink (SK)

*Use 15cm (6") round or square cake recipe

EQUIPMENT

20cm (8") and 35cm (14") round cake boards (drums)

Large and small rolling pins

Cake smoother

Plain-bladed knife

Palette knife

Ruler

Paintbrushes: no. 2 (for glue), no. 0 (for painting) and no. 6 (for dusting)

Scissors

Serrated carving knife

Cake leveller

10mm (³/₈"), 15mm (⁵/₈") and 18mm (¾") circle cutters

Food-grade foam sponge

Piping nozzles: nos. 1.5 and 2

Jacket template (see page 108)

Parchment paper piping bags

Cocktail sticks

Glass cake stand/separator, 20-25cm (8-10") tall

Ribbon: pale lilac (to trim cake board)

Non-toxic glue stick

Note

With this particular design, if using marzipan on the large round cake, cover top of the cake first, then roll out a strip to cover the sides (see pages 21 to 22). This will create a sharp edge around the top of the cake ready for the sugarpaste covering.

A Fine Romance

This has to be the most romantic of wedding cakes, with Romeo on his knees before his Juliet.

METHOD

Board

1 Roll out 500g (1lb 1¾oz) of white sugarpaste to a thickness of 2-3mm (under ¹/₈") and cover the large cake board (drum). Polish the surface with a cake smoother to remove any imperfections and create a smooth surface and then trim away any excess paste from around the edge. Cover the smaller cake board in the same way using 300g (10½oz) of sugarpaste and then set both aside to dry.

Cakes

2 Position the largest cake towards the back of the large cake board with a little filling underneath to secure (the filling is not required if using marzipan-covered rich fruit cakes).

3 Cover the sides of the cake first. If using sponge cakes, rework the crumb coat with a palette knife or add a little more cake filling to the surface to help the sugarpaste stick. For rich fruit cakes, brush the marzipan surface with a little clear alcohol. Knead 700g (1lb 8¾oz) of white sugarpaste until soft and pliable. Roll out to a thickness of 3-4mm (¹/₈") and cut a strip measuring the depth of the cake and at least 75cm (29½") in length. Sprinkle with icing sugar to prevent sticking and roll up. Position against the side of the cake and unroll around the cake, securing the join closed with a little

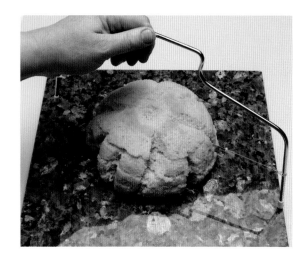

edible glue. Gently rub the surface with a cake smoother. Indent lines using a ruler, 1cm (³/₈") apart and mark vertical lines for a brick effect. Brush along the lines with a damp paintbrush to soften the edges.

4 To cover the top of the cake, roll out 500g (1lb 1¾oz) of white sugarpaste to a circle with a 28cm (11") diameter, lift with the rolling pin and place on top of the cake. Cut a neat edge using scissors and then smooth with your fingers to round off the cut edge. Smooth the surface with cake smoother.

5 To make the top tier dress, trim the crust from the bowl-shaped cake and level the top. Cut vertical wedges from the surface to create pleats. If using a sponge cake, cut layers using the cake leveller and sandwich together with cake filling. Spread a layer over the surface of the cake as a crumb coat and to help the sugarpaste stick. For a rich fruit cake,

brush the surface of the carved cake with apricot glaze and cover with marzipan. Brush with clear alcohol just before covering with sugarpaste. Position the cake slightly off-centre on the cake board. If using a sponge cake, use a dab of cake filling to secure the cake in place.

6 To cover the dress, roll out 450g (1lb) of white sugarpaste and cover the cake completely. Smooth the paste downwards over the shape of the cake and trim off the excess paste from around the base. Pinch to exaggerate the pleats around the top and push into the centre to make a dip ready for the bodice.

Steps

7 Thickly roll out 300g (10½oz) of white sugarpaste and cut a strip for the top step measuring 25cm (10") in length, 3cm (1¼") wide and 4.5cm (1¾") deep. Using

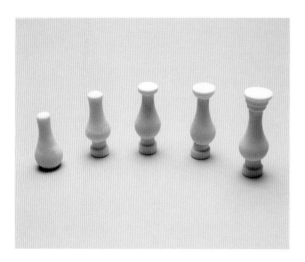

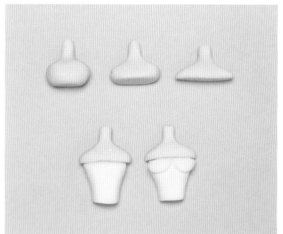

the remaining white sugarpaste, cut another strip to the same length, 2cm (¾") wide and 2cm (¾") deep. Stick these in position against the front of the cake. Roll out some white modelling paste and cut strips to cover the top of each step, overlapping slightly at the front.

8   For the step sides, roll out 125g (4½oz) of white modelling paste to a thickness of 1.5cm (just over ½") and cut two 6cm (2³/₈") squares. Cut a dip into each for the front part and indent using the back of a knife. Stick in position at either end of the steps.

Balustrade

9   Model all the pieces to build up the balustrade next to allow for drying time. Make each piece individually from white modelling paste and build up as illustrated in the step picture using the different sized circle cutters.

Make 27 pillars altogether and then set aside to dry.

Bodice

10   To make the bodice, roll 10g (¼oz) of white modelling paste into a teardrop shape, press down to flatten slightly and cut the top and bottom straight. Model the neck and chest using 5g (just under ¼oz) of flesh tone modelling paste, following the step picture as a guide. Stick the two pieces together using edible glue. Roll a small ball of white, press down to flatten slightly and cut in half. Stick in position on either side of the bodice.

11   Using a little edible glue, stick the body onto the dress. Support the neck and gently push a sugar stick down through the neck and into the body, leaving at least 1cm (³/₈") protruding to help hold the head in place later.

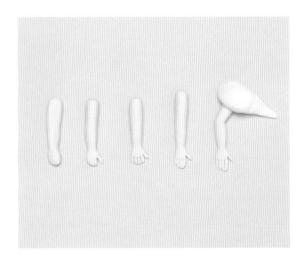

Bride's Arms

12 Split 5g (just under ¼oz) of flesh tone modelling paste in half and model the two arms, using the step picture as a guide. Model a teardrop-shaped sleeve and then secure the arms in position on the figure. Mark pleats using the paintbrush handle, smoothing each sleeve into the centre of the bodice and finishing with a tiny ball of white paste. Cut a tiny strip to edge the bottom of each sleeve and glue in place.

Heads

13 Split 15g (½oz) of flesh tone modelling paste in half. Roll both halves into ball shapes for the heads. Stroke gently down the facial area to flatten slightly and smooth the paste down, pinching gently on either side to shape the chin. Carefully push one head down onto the sugar stick and secure with a little edible glue. Roll tiny ball noses and stick in position slightly below the centre. To create the man's open mouth, push the end of a paintbrush gently into the paste.

Groom

14 To make the groom's trousers, roll 50g (1¾oz) of dark grey modelling paste into a sausage and press to flatten slightly. Make a cut three quarters along the length to separate the legs and then round off the cut edges. Using the step photograph as a guide, bend into the kneeling pose. Use a piece of food-grade foam sponge to support the upright leg until dry. Split the black modelling paste in half and make the shoes. Mark the heels on the bottom and secure to the legs with edible glue.

15 For the shirt, roll 15g (½oz) of white modelling paste into a sausage shape and glue in

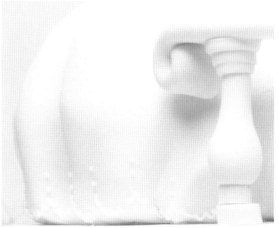

position on top of the trousers. Thinly roll out some pale grey modelling paste and cut out the waistcoat. Mark down the centre with a knife. Stick in position and add tiny buttons cut from the no. 2 piping nozzle.

16 Thinly roll out some dark grey modelling paste and cut out the jacket using the template. Stick in position around the man's body. Split 15g (½oz) of dark grey paste in half and use to make the sleeves, indent halfway and bend at the elbow. Stick in position, supported in the pose with pieces of food-grade foam sponge. Cut a strip of dark grey modelling paste for the jacket collar. Cut two small jacket pockets and a tiny strip for the top of the 'v' at the base of the jacket. Stick tiny buttons on the jacket cut from the no. 1.5 piping nozzle.

17 Roll two pea-sized balls of white paste for cuffs and indent the centre of each with the end

of a paintbrush. Thinly roll out some more white, cut two triangles for the turned-up collar and pleat a small piece for the cravat. Secure the pieces in place with edible glue.

18 To make the groom's hands, use pea-sized amounts of flesh tone modelling paste and follow the step picture for the bride. Moisten inside the cuffs with edible glue a few minutes before positioning the hands as the glue will be tacky and the hands will stick more easily.

Decoration

19 Place some white royal icing in a piping bag with the no. 1.5 piping nozzle and pipe the looped pattern around the base of the dress.

20 Arrange the balustrade in position, ensuring that the pillars are evenly spaced – use seven for the top tier and 20 for the large round cake. Secure in place

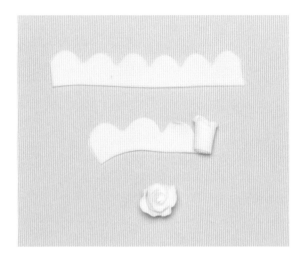

with dabs of royal icing. Roll 35g (1¼oz) of white modelling paste into a sausage measuring 25cm (10") in length. Press flat and then curl each end under into a spiral. Stick this in position to complete the balustrade on the top tier. Repeat for the large cake using 115g (4oz) and roll to a length of 75cm (29½").

21 Make the roses next using the remaining white modelling paste. To make a rose, roll a small ball, about the size of two garden peas put together. Roll this into a sausage shape and press flat. Press along one edge with your fingertip, gently stroking out a scalloped edge. Turn the strip over and moisten the straight bottom edge with a little edible glue. Gently roll this strip into a spiral and then pinch at the bottom to narrow the base of the rose and push out the petals at the top. If needed, use a paintbrush to gently fan out the petals. Pick each rose up by pushing

into the centre with a cocktail stick when complete and stick in position with a little royal icing. Using a piping bag fitted with the no. 1.5 piping nozzle and filled with pale green royal icing, pipe the vines. For the leaves, cut a small 'v' from the tip of a piping bag and pipe leaves in groups along the vines. The point of the 'v' shapes the central leaf vein.

Hair

22 Using the brown royal icing in a piping bag with the no. 1.5 piping nozzle, pipe the bride's hair. Attach the royal icing to the top of her head by squeezing gently on the piping bag and then, keeping an even pressure, draw the tip downwards and into the nape of her neck. Build up the hair little by little and then pipe her ponytail. Use a cocktail stick to indent the parting and then add a rose to her hair. Pipe the man's hair using light brown royal icing.

To Finish

23 Using black and red liquid food colouring and a fine paintbrush, paint the facial details onto both figures.

Top Tip

If you make any mistakes when painting, carefully wipe away the colour with a clean, damp brush and paint again.

24 Trim both cake boards with pale lilac ribbon, securing with a non-toxic glue stick. Place the top tier onto a glass separator, next to the lower tier.

25 Dust the cake, dress and roses with pink dust colour using the no. 6 paintbrush. Add a little pink colour to the bride's cheeks.

Romantic mini cakes

To elevate each mini cake, thickly roll out some white modelling paste and cut circles slightly larger than the thin mini cake boards on which each cake will sit. Leave to dry completely before positioning the cakes on the centre of each. You can team these stylish pedestal mini cakes with simple cupcakes decorated with a circle of small rolled roses.

MATERIALS

3 prepared round cakes (filled and crumb-coated, or marzipan-covered rich fruit cakes) in following sizes:

>25cm (10"), 8cm (3") depth; 20cm (8"), 8cm (3") depth; 15cm (6"), 8cm (3") depth

30-45ml (2-3tbsp) clear alcohol (only required if using marzipan)

Sugarpaste:

>500g (1lb 1¾oz) black; 1kg (2lb 3¼oz) red ; 1.25kg (2lb 12oz) white

Modelling paste:

>315g (11oz) black; pea-sized amount of pale green; 90g (3oz) red; 240g (8½oz) white

Icing sugar in a sugar shaker

Edible glue (SK)

2 sugar sticks, 5-10cm (2-4") in length (see page 25) or raw, dried spaghetti

Liquid food colours or diluted paste food colours: black and red (SK)

EQUIPMENT

35cm (14") round cake board (drum), 20cm (8") and 15cm (6") thin round cake cards or food-grade foam board

Large and small rolling pins

Cake smoother

Plain-bladed knife

Palette knife

Plastic food-grade dowelling rods

Pencil

Paintbrushes: no. 2 (for glue); nos. 0 and 2 (for painting)

Cocktail stick

Miniature heart cutter

Blossom plunger cutter set

Plain piping nozzles: nos. 1.5, 3 and 16 (PME)

Cake separator

Spotty ribbon: black and white (to trim cake board)

Non-toxic glue stick

Feline Fantasy

With a bold combination of red, white and black, this appealing design is certainly eye-catching. The unusual cake top was influenced by the beauty and elegance of Siamese cats and the hand painted scrolls and curls by the fantasy art of Asia.

METHOD

Board

1 Roll out the black sugarpaste to a depth of 2-3mm (under ⅛") and cover the cake board. Polish the surface with a cake smoother to remove any imperfections and achieve a smooth surface and then trim away the excess paste from around the edge. Set aside to dry.

Cakes

2 Position the largest cake centrally on the cake board with a little filling underneath to secure (the filling is not required if using marzipan-covered rich fruit cakes).

3 Before covering the bottom tier with sugarpaste, rework the crumb coat using a palette knife or add a little more cake filling to the surface to help the sugarpaste stick. For a rich fruit cake, brush the marzipan surface with a little clear alcohol. Knead the red sugarpaste until soft and pliable. Roll to a thickness of 3-4mm (⅛") and use to cover the base cake completely, carefully stretching out any pleats and smoothing down and around the shape with the palm of your hand. Rub the surface with a cake smoother and then trim away any excess paste from around the base.

4 Place the two remaining tiers on the corresponding cake cards, trimming the cards to fit the circumference of the cakes if necessary. Cover both cakes with white sugarpaste.

5 To ensure the cakes are well supported, you will need to dowel the base and middle tiers (see instructions on page 25). Insert five dowels, evenly spaced in a circle, into the cake on the cake board, mark with a pencil, remove and cut to size. Insert the dowels back into the holes in the cake so that they are level with the cake top.

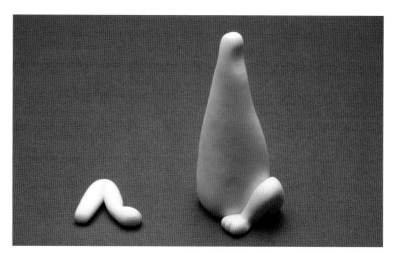

6   Carefully position the second tier centrally on top of the bottom tier. Dowel this cake with three dowelling rods, keeping three dowels near the centre to support the cake separator, which will support the top tier.

Cats

7   To make the white cat, model the body shape first using 90g (3oz) of white modelling paste. Knead the paste until it is smooth and crack-free and then roll into a long teardrop shape. Gently pinch the narrow end, bringing the paste up to form a slender neck. If you place this body upright too soon the weight will cause the paste to sink, so lie it flat for 5 to 10 minutes to allow the paste to firm up slightly. Roll gently over the surface to remove the flattened area where the body has lain, then stand the body upright. Push in on one side to indent the small of the back and round off the bottom.

8   Push a large sugar stick (or strand of spaghetti) down through the neck, leaving at least 1cm (³/₈") protruding to help hold the head in position.

9   To make the chest, roll 10g (¼oz) of white modelling paste into a teardrop shape and press to flatten. Smooth over the surface and thin out the paste around the edge. Cut a 'v' shape into the full end and then pinch the top to follow the shape of the neck. Smooth once again and stick in position at the front of the body using edible glue. The 'v' should reach around mid-way on the body.

10   For the legs, split 60g (2oz) of white modelling paste into four equal pieces. To make a leg, roll one piece into a sausage shape and round off one end for the paw. Push down on the paw to bring it forward and then mark lines along the front using a knife. For the back legs, bend the leg in the middle and stick either side at the base of the cat. Smooth the top of the front legs so the shape follows the contours of the chest area, secure in position and then slightly blend in either side by rubbing gently over the surface.

11   For the head, roll a 30g (1oz) ball of white modelling paste and pinch out the muzzle, turning it up slightly. Indent a line from the tip downwards using the back of a knife. Push the head gently into position on the body, slightly tilted and supported by the sugar stick.

12   To make the eyes, roll two small, pea-sized balls of white modelling paste and squeeze both sides to make a pointed oval (boat) shape. Brush the back with

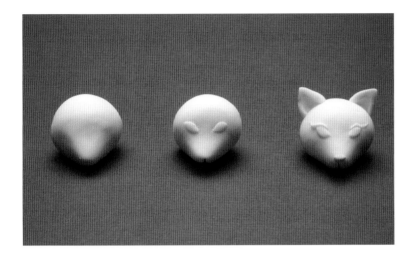

edible glue and stick in position so that they are tilted upwards. Stick a tiny ball of pale green paste onto the centre of each and press flat, smoothing out until the iris reaches the top and bottom edges of the eye. Roll two tiny, tapered sausage shapes to edge the top of each eye, tilting each one up on the outer corners.

13 Knead a tiny amount of red modelling paste into white to make a reddish-pink shade. Model an oval-shaped nose, indent the base and mark the nostrils using the end of a paintbrush. Mark a few holes for whiskers using the tip of a cocktail stick.

14 For the ears, roll two pea-sized amounts of white modelling paste into teardrop shapes and indent into the centre of each by rolling the end of a paintbrush into the surface. Cut the rounded end straight and stick the

ears in position using a little edible glue.

15 Roll a sausage shape for the tail using 10g (¼oz) of white modelling paste, curl and stick in place.

16 Make the black cat in the same way as before, keeping the pose slightly more upright. For this cat you will need to use 100g (1½oz) of black modelling paste for his body, 10g (¼oz) for the chest, 65g (2¼oz) split into four pieces for the legs, 30g (1oz) for his head and the remainder for his tail and ears.

Pattern

17 Using the black and red liquid (or diluted paste) food colours and no. 0 and 2 paintbrushes, paint the scrolls, lines and curls around the base of the bottom two tiers.

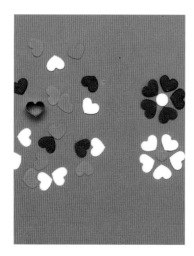

18 Paint the eyes, eyelashes and fine lines for whiskers on the cats using the no. 0 paintbrush and black liquid food colour.

19 Thinly roll out any remaining red, white and black modelling paste and cut out hearts, blossoms and circles (using piping nozzles) to make the patterns around the cake. Stick a red blossom to the white cat's ear.

20 Place the separator in the centre of the middle tier and place the top tier in position. Place the cats on top. Trim the base board with spotty ribbon.

Mini fantasy cakes

I used round and square shapes here, keeping the round shapes similar in decoration to the main cake and the square shapes more formally decorated. I like to mix different shapes together so a quick and easy idea would be to make some heart shaped cakes covered with red sugarpaste and kept plain. These would look stunning and complement the other designs beautifully.

Templates

Butterflies for Lace Butterflies, pages 36 to 41.

Door and bell tower for New England Chapel, pages 28 to 35.

Eyes for Ganesh's Blessing, pages 72 to 79.

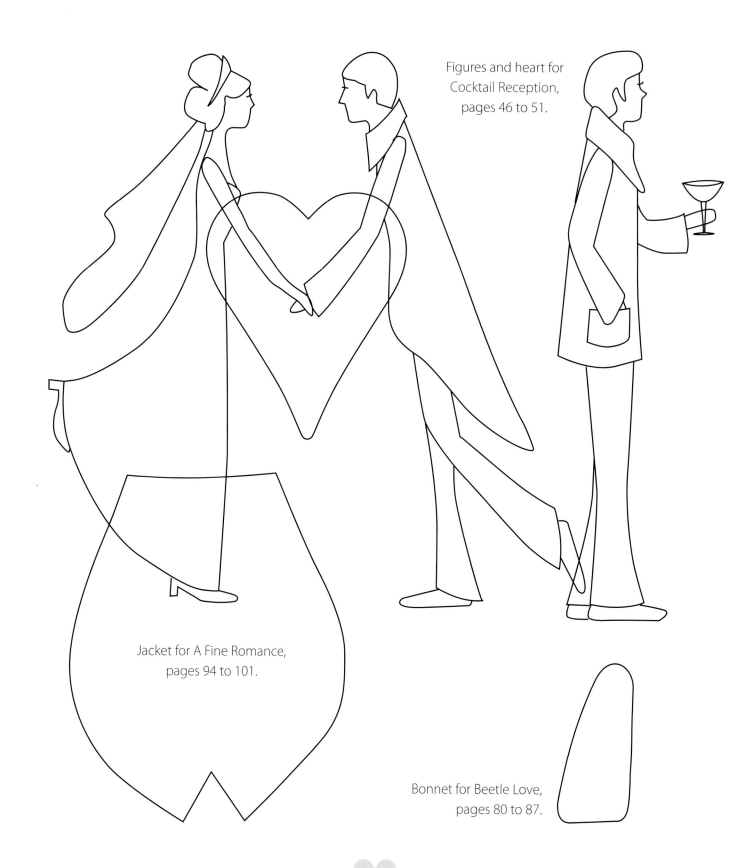

Figures and heart for
Cocktail Reception,
pages 46 to 51.

Jacket for A Fine Romance,
pages 94 to 101.

Bonnet for Beetle Love,
pages 80 to 87.

Plane pieces for
Flying High, pages
66 to 71.

Clothing for Mouse Party,
pages 58 to 65.

Backdrop and lettering for 60s Love,
pages 52 to 57.

Wording, music and
violin for Wedding
March, pages 88 to 93.

with the
groom by
her side

Suppliers

Shops

UK

♥ Jane Asher Party Cakes
24 Cale Street
London SW3 3QU
Tel: 020 7584 6177
Fax: 020 7584 6179
E-mail: info@janeasher.com
Website: www.jane-asher.co.uk

♥ Pipedreams
2 Bell Lane
Eton Wick
Windsor
Berkshire
SL4 6JP
Tel/Fax: 01753 865682
E-mail:
pipedreaming@btinternet.com
Website:
www.pipedreams-sugarcraft.co.uk

♥ Squires Kitchen Sugarcraft (SK)
Squires House
3 Waverley Lane
Farnham
Surrey
GU9 8BB
Tel: 0845 22 55 67 1/2 (from UK)
+44 (0)1252 711749 (from overseas)
E-mail: customer@squires-shop.com
Websites: www.squires-shop.com
www.squiresschool.co.uk

♥ Sugar Celebrations
37 Faringdon Road
Swindon
Wiltshire
SN1 5AR
Tel: 01793 513549
and
80 Westgate Street
Gloucester
GL1 2NZ
Tel: 01452 308848
E-mail: girls@sugarcelebrations.com
Website: www.sugarcelebrations.com

Australia

♥ Cakedeco
Shop 7
Port Phillip Arcade
228 Flinders Street
Melbourne
Australia
T: +61 (0) 3 9654 5335
cakedeco@optusnet.com.au

♥ Iced Affair
53 Church St.
Camperdown
NSW 2050
Australia
T: +61 (0) 2 9519 3679
icedaffair@iprimus.com.au
Website: www.icedaffair.com.au

♥ Susie Q Cake Decorating
Centre
Shop 4
372 Keilor Road
Niddrie
Victoria 3042
Australia
Tel: +61 (0) 3 9379 2275
Website: www.susie-qcake.com.au

The Netherlands

♥ Planet Cake®
Zuidplein 117
3083 CN
Rotterdam
The Netherlands
Tel: +31 (0)10 290 91 30
E-mail: info@cake.nl
Website: www.cake.nl

Sweden

♥ Tårtdecor
Bultgatan 14
442 40 KUNGÄLV
Svierge
Tel: +46 303 514 70
E-mail: info@tartdecor.se
Website: www.tartdecor.se

Manufacturers and Distributors

UK

♥ Ceefor Cakes
PO Box 443
Leighton Buzzard
Bedfordshire
LU7 1AJ
Tel: 01525 375237
Fax: 01525 385414
E-mail: info@ceeforcakes.co.uk
Website: www.ceeforcakes.co.uk

♥ Confectionery Supplies
Unit 11a, b and c
Foley Trading Estate
Hereford
HR1 2SF
Tel: 01432 371451
029 2037 2161 (mail order)
E-mail: kclements@btinternet.com
Website:
www.confectionerysupplies.co.uk

♥ Design Acrylics
28 The Green
Mountsorrel
Leicester
LE12 7AF
E-mail: designacrylics@gmail.com

♥ Guy, Paul & Co. Ltd.
Unit 10, The Business Centre
Corinium Industrial Estate
Raans Road
Amersham
Buckinghamshire
HP6 6FB
Tel: 01494 432121
E-mail: sales@guypaul.co.uk
Website: www.guypaul.co.uk

♥ Renshaw
Crown Street
Liverpool
L8 7RF
E-mail: enquiries@renshaw-nbf.co.uk
Website: www.renshaw-nbf.co.uk

♥ Squires Group
Squires House
3 Waverley Lane
Farnham
Surrey
GU9 8BB
Tel: 0845 22 55 67 1/2 (from UK)
+44 (0)1252 711749 (from overseas)
E-mail: info@squires-group.co.uk
Websites: www.squires-group.co.uk
www.cakesandsugarcraft.co.uk
www.squires-exhibition.co.uk

USA

♥ Caljava International School
of Cake Decorating and Sugar
Craft
19519 Business Center Drive
Northridge, CA 91324
USA
Tel: +1 818 718 2707
Fax: +1 818 718 2715
E-mail: caljava@aol.com
Website: www.cakevisions.com

♥ Beryl's Cake Decorating &
Pastry Supplies
PO Box 1584
N. Springfield, VA
USA
Tel: +1 800 488 2749
Website: www.beryls.com

Guilds

♥ The British Sugarcraft Guild
Wellington House
Messeter Place
London
SE9 5DP
Tel: 020 8859 6943
Website: www.bsguk.org